BROKEN

Tales of a Titanium Cowgirl

BROKEN

Tales of a Titanium Cowgirl

Michelle R. Scully

SPINNING SEVENS
PRESS

SPINNING SEVENS
PRESS

ISBN 978-0-9992465-0-4
Cover photo by Nathan Dehart/ nathandehart.com
Cover designed by Emily Kitching.

Dedication

Dedicated to my BLM mustang Luke, who taught us that you should always listen to your horse, even if it takes you a long time to figure that out.

Contents

Foreword

Broken. The title gave me the willies—until I read the subtitle: *Tales of a Titanium Cowgirl.*

Broken. That single word, especially when you live in a horse-centric world, connotes catastrophic consequences and makes even the strongest cowperson wince. But what a beautiful, gutsy, and flip reply to the title the subtitle is: *Tales of a Titanium Cowgirl.*

In so few words Michelle Scully, in her gifted way, produced in me at once grave concern and chuckling, and had me visualizing the kind of tenacious, good natured women I have come to admire in the rural country that I know.

Immediately it was obvious that whatever wreck had happened at the heart of this story, it was not a simple one. But, regardless of its severity, the calamity was not going to get our heroine down. That subtitle proved to be a promise—the subtitle mocked the title, daring it to keep a grip on the narrator through what was about to unfold in the pages that followed.

Titanium is really tough, and everyone knows, so are cowgirls—just imagine the bionic woman that emerges when the two combine! I had to jump into the manuscript and see what was going on here. I was not let down. Michelle seemed effortlessly to deliver chapter after chapter of an engaging story, deadly serious in its subject, but free from doom and gloom, with a sharp wit and often wry humor that had me hooked.

Broken, Tales of a Titanium Cowgirl is not just an autobiographical account of a terrible horse wreck. It is as much a book about life, overcoming trauma, and getting one's world into perspective again after crossing, as Michelle so aptly puts it, one of life's "black Sharpie lines."

For those of us who have fallen flat across a black Sharpie line in the past, we can see Michelle gets it right in this book. The phases of realities that catch up with you, the fears, the family dynamics—she gets down the brass tacks of the experience in a most authentic way.

Even though tripping over a black Sharpie line is not a deal I care to dwell on these days, I thoroughly enjoyed reading this book. One of the main reasons is Michelle's natural sense of humor. Humor is an essential element in finding the joys in life and for healing from the insults that wound us. And, when we can laugh at ourselves, it puts our tiny realities in this huge universe a little more in perspective.

And then there are the horses.

Horses. Horse obsession is a unique disorder. The horse obsessed will understand immediately how Michelle longs to get back to see her horses after the accident...how she burns inside to ride again when a reasonably sane person might have had enough of horses after such a wreck. But horses are horses, and Michelle never blames her horse for her difficulties, and she loves her/them as much as ever. Seeking to ride again for Michelle really is just putting the world back into its proper orbit after being knocked off course. Oh horses!

From the first chapter I knew this was a special book. Special not because of its extraordinariness—it is beautifully simple, really—but special because of its honesty and brilliant good humor, especially in the face of calamitous, life altering circumstances. Anyone can relate to Michelle. Who doesn't cheer on the underdog, especially when she is cracking a joke in the face of overwhelming odds? Michelle's faith, love, and candid, reflective nature, truly do turn a story about being badly *Broken* into the triumph of *Tales of a Titanium Cowgirl*.

Tom Moates
July 2017

Acknowledgements

With love to Pat, Max, and Jake. You three are my heart.
With love and gratitude for my family, friends, and faith.
To Scout, Kai and Clementine, Satin, Simba, Sundance and Wish –
all the animals we live with and all the others who graciously share
their beautiful habitat with us. They make me smile and bless me
every day with their grounding presence.

And with thanks to Tom Moates, for believing in *Broken* and for
being as horse crazy as I am (or maybe more).

Introduction

My life has zigged and zagged in and out of horses, and thankfully they zigged back in for good about fifteen years ago. Horses fuel my soul. Riding was something I'd done my whole life, but stumbling across something called horsemanship was a new world. There was a good and a not-so-good side to my discovery – I'd found a place where others with the same passion for horses had congregated, but on the flip side I found myself standing in the middle of a round pen thinking *I don't know a bleeping thing about horses.* Although I'd spent a good part of my life around horses, the more I learned about the quest we call horsemanship, the more I realized I had been kind of clueless.

Five-year old me was much more intuitive and focused on what my horse thought than older-me who wanted to go fast, play

Harry Whitney makes it all look so easy. There's float in the line and Harry and Satin are having a nice conversation.

polo, rope – *do* things on a horse. This brave new world was behind this door I had opened and when I entered it I felt like the least knowledgeable person at the party. Now I had a glimpse of how it looked to do things with a horse (like five-year old me), to have their thought with you, to interact as partners. It was a way of being with horses and not chasing a horse around trying to get him to do things, but instead asking, and instead, offering.

Even though I'd seen a new way, it still took some time to figure out whom to learn from. Clinics can be pretty overwhelming, especially depending on the format and the horseman. In the horse world, just like any other, there are those who are there to sell. Even under that big tent, there are some who are more showman than horseman. One of the first clinics I attended had people crying in the arena and leaving in the middle of the night. It was pretty intense for one of my first forays into clinics and I was feeling pretty stressed out about being there. My gelding Skeeter was feeling stressed out too, but I didn't have enough confidence in my own instincts to load him up and just take us both home. I should have. I waded through a few detours before I found a core group of horsemen and women I want to be learning from and I made friends with other people who are on that same path. When you find yourself in the presence of someone who is all in for the horse, you just feel the truth in it.

I'd never imagined that the old saying "When you fall off a horse, you've got to get back on" would become literal for me. Independence was always my cornerstone (and sometimes to a fault) and my previous broken bones paled in comparison to the sense of utter decimation I felt when I learned that my back was broken so badly that it would be my own miracle if I could be put back together again without permanent impairment. Little did I know upon receiving that diagnosis that my faith, love for horses, and horsemanship journey would converge so powerfully to help me find my way through a very scary, dark time. I started writing *Broken, Tales of a Titanium Cowgirl* to help my spirit heal after my wreck. Unfortunately my expectations of when I would be "healed" were way off base. I had no idea how long it would take until my body and soul didn't feel taped together (with very flimsy tape) or to be able to sleep through the night without anxiety. I had absolutely no idea how I would actually get back on a horse. I knew I wanted to, but wanting to and doing were just so far apart. I just knew, whether it was a goal I set to make myself feel better or not, I would ride again. Sometimes it's those

Satin and I having a lively, intentional walk-around.

things we never expected that lead us on a journey of healing, discovery, and, believe it or not, wonder.

It might not be a horse you came off, but I'd venture a guess that life has thrown you in a way you never saw coming a time or two. Thank you for opening this book and taking this journey with me. My hope is that if you are figuring out your own unexpected journey, you'll walk with me a bit through mine and perhaps my story can help encourage you should you find yourself navigating through some unfamiliar terrain of your own. May you find your way out of the valley and into the sunshine. May your path be scattered with love, faith, friendship, birds, dogs, and of course horses. Always horses. Happy (and unexpected) trails!

Photo Credits

All photo credits are to Michelle R. Scully except for the following:

Chapter One

An Unfortunate Dismount

I can't change the direction of the wind. But I can adjust my sails.
Jimmy Dean

I'd never paid much attention to the Chinese New Year but I'm starting to think maybe I'd better. 2011 was the Chinese Year of the Rabbit. Truth be told, when 2011 rolled around I wasn't thinking about the new year at all as I was still wondering what had happened to 2010. The Year of the Rabbit caught my attention when my adventure as a newly-minted titanium cowgirl sprang directly from an unfortunate interaction with a rabbit in early 2011, changing my life in the veritable blink of an eye. My friend Colleen is a farmer and, as all farmers must, she accepts the vagaries of weather, worry, and life. We became friends because our families share a livelihood; we are very similar in many ways, and appreciate that about each other. We live in a small rural community, and even here where people have known each other for generations, people are constantly thinking I am her and she is me. Even her father thinks we look alike. Fortunately our husbands can tell the difference. Farmers have a unique wisdom borne from a life wedded to the earth and the uncertainties inherent in earning a living by coaxing plants out of the soil and, hopefully, into a harvest. We were talking one day and she said something I've never forgotten. "Life can change in the blink of an eye, but it's in that same blink that God works." She knows what she's talking about in lots of things, and she's spot on about this.

We can all identify our own moment, that blink of an eye drawing an indelible black Sharpie line between "before" and what comes "after." The unexpected jolt of the phone ringing in the middle of the night waking you from your sleep with a cold chill in your bones....the text that says "Mom, I messed up...." The news that someone you believed imperishable is gone. Usually the "after" is the loss and grief that hits us unaware when we were happily minding our own busy-ness and not paying attention to our moments. My black Sharpie moment began when the beautiful, unseasonable warmth of a winter afternoon in late January called me out for a spur of the moment ride shortly before dark. The winter had been incessantly wet and cold and not much riding had happened since the Mark Rashid clinic I'd attended in late November. This ride would be my first real ride since. My goal was to see where my mare Wichado's ("Wish") mind was since the clinic and take it from there. No big plans, no expectations, just going with the moment. Or so I told myself. It's a fine irony that some of our most significant life experiences start off with hopeful serendipity. I guess the point of serendipity is that we don't know the outcome before we begin.

I grabbed my gear, drove down to the barn in the four-wheeler and brought Wish out of the pasture to saddle. Have you ever noticed how much better a horse warmed by sunshine smells than one who's been muddy all winter? The smell of a sunshine-warm horse is therapeutic. Wish was calm and soft and we set off moving fluidly down the hill for a little ride around what my family calls the animal superhighway. The superhighway is a naturally-worn path around the hill in the center of our property worn into a trail used by the animals that use it in their daily travels. Crisscrossed with turkey and coyote tracks and coyote poop; the animal superhighway is a gold-mine of animal activity. Sometimes we spend so much time looking down at the path to see whether the big bucks are out and about yet (their hoof prints are distinctive) or if the coyotes are eating from the vineyards during harvest (the grapes in their poop give them away), that we lose sight of where we're going and end up in the manzanita. It's a super interesting superhighway. The late afternoon was golden warm for January when the warmth of the sun is unexpected and all the more appreciated.

Wish and I were in the zone, moving out in an easy way. Wish was enjoying the ride as much as I was. She was, until we came to a part of the trail where some obstacles bothered her and her mind left me and got stuck on the obstacles. If I could hit the rewind button, I could see that she had given me signs that her mind had left when we got to the meadow and her mind was still not really with me. My mind started thinking "It's getting dark, we need to get going" rather than turning my own mind in the right direction to help get her thought back with me. Instead, I skipped past doing what needed doing and my thought was focused on the sun's fading and night coming. So much for being in the moment. Using all the super powers of hindsight, it's obvious to me that I should have taken her at her word, but I didn't transition from my own desire to "just ride" to meet her where she needed me to. I ignored that, and I got lulled into the lure of taking a lope too shortly after that. She was more than willing to go, which was clue number two, but the wild backyard riding kid in me overwhelmed the budding horseman in me and I took what she gave me, and we went.

Fast.

That stolen lope might have worked out okay if that damn rabbit hadn't bolted right through her legs, like something out of a bad cartoon. Where's Elmer freakin' Fudd when you really need him? All those awful old cartoons of Elmer Fudd fighting endlessly with Bugs Bunny made a little more sense now. I can still see it unfolding in a slow motion loop in my mind, seeing the rabbit out of the corner of my left eye and realizing it was hauling some major rabbit butt and right for us. That rabbit ended up so unnaturally close to Wish's leading foot that she would have kicked the long-eared trouble maker if she hadn't chosen the alternate course of action of shooting up into the air like a rocket and sideways, simultaneously. Her rapid-rabbit response left me with what seemed like only two options: careening into the tree now in front of me or bailing off. Obviously bailing off was best? I hadn't really thought through the ramifications other than I knew that at that point my choices were limited. In my mind's eye I saw myself pulling this off by dismounting with a masterful Ninja roll, or at the very least, some stylish landing. Living in a predominately testosterone-influenced environment as I do gives me lots of exposure to action films and Ninjas and super heroes. In real life though, I'm not a Ninja and the roll I had imagined consisted instead of a mid-air flip over on to my back and what felt like a very slow, long drop to the hard ground from what seemed like an incredibly high distance.

And then, silence.

Not even my breath.

I lay in the center of the superhighway. I was trying to do a check list on myself to ascertain damage but my mind was reeling. I had heard a loud "pop" when I hit the ground and a wave of pain hit me like a hammer. I didn't taste blood. I was still conscious. Both good things. When I could breathe again, I rolled over and tried to stand. The pain was blinding. I tried to catch my breath and clear my head. It was starting to get dark, no one knew exactly where I was, and I hadn't been smart enough to bring my cell phone. Or to wear the new helmet my folks bought me for Christmas. I fought the panic and tried to clear my head enough to formulate a plan. The choices seemed few and the distance from me to the house seemed like a million miles. Somehow I set my mind to crawling and I did. I often walk that same path and distance now and can't fathom how I managed a yard, let alone what was probably almost half a mile. Somehow I got to the top of the hill and to the quad and crawled in. I found Wish standing next to it, waiting for help. Somehow I got the gate open and let her in. Horse people understand why I felt compelled to make sure she was okay; non-horse people and mothers don't.

Somehow I crawled back into the quad and headed up to the house, hunched over the steering wheel, not really sure what I was thinking other than I just wanted it to be over and to lie down anywhere other than on the superhighway in the coming dark. I crawled up to the house, knocked on the door. My son Jake answered. As I crawled into the house he looked at me trying to process what he was seeing. "Mom, what can I do?" "Honey, call your dad." Moments later I heard my husband's truck tearing up the drive and saw his look of uncertainty as he flew through the door. "What happened? Are you okay?" I told him "I don't think I'm going to feel too good tomorrow."

Because I've always been overly and sometimes ridiculously optimistic, we had a conversation about whether or not to call the ambulance. When I told him about the loud pop that was my first clue that no good had come from my untimely dismount, he called 911. The ambulance came tearing up our gravel drive and they loaded me up and into the back and off we went. A blink of an eye, a black Sharpie line forever dividing before and after. Sometimes we don't even know the line is there until we begin the journey.

I could say the rabbit started it all, but did it really? That was mine to figure out. The Year of the Rabbit is said to represent a placid year, following after the ferocious Year of the Tiger. I remain unconvinced. My rabbit was proving to be pretty ferocious, and we were just getting acquainted.

Chapter Two

Can Do Girls: Is crawling really an option?

Plodding wins the race.
Aesop

My country girlfriends get it. We call it being a can-do girl as in, "I can do that, now get out of the way" kind of way. Living in the country lends itself to figuring things out and no shortage of things to fix. It's amazing the things you can fix with just duct tape and baling twine. There's definitely an upside to being can-do, but sometimes it makes it harder to recognize when you should not. When word spread about my accident, and more sensationally, that I'd crawled home, eighth-grade boys were impressed but my neurosurgeon, not so much. The count was country girls thinking "yes, crawling was an option"; the sane people like my doctor and mom were thinking "not so much."

We watched rodeo for years and looked forward to going to the National Finals Rodeo in Las Vegas every year. Without fail, a bull rider or two get thrown, stepped on, and pummeled so badly you can hardly believe they can stand, but they do. They pop up and leave the arena without assistance, but just barely. The crowd claps. We like that they get right back up after they get thrown. We don't see what happens after and can only wonder if they collapse as soon as they're out of the arena. Adrenaline mixed with fear is a potent cocktail, causing your mind to go code-black into survival mode. Can-do goes pretty deep if it's in your bones and I'd just learned it works on autopilot too.

Moments after my wreck I was in big-time shock, which is abundantly clear to me now, but the mind goes places of its own accord in the aftermath of an accident. Now I think back to finding myself lying in the middle of the superhighway, and considering my options. Like a frightened animal, I was desperate to get to safety. I didn't know when I'd be found. I also wanted to find Wish and make sure she was okay. I dreaded her stepping on her reins and tearing her mouth. Dark was falling and since I had tried to walk and could not, crawling had seemed the most immediate solution, so I began. I just kept crawling until I reached the top. Crazy thoughts, but they seemed to make sense with the cocktail of adrenaline and fear I was high on.

Hands, then knees.

Hands then knees, I kept telling myself, a million times. I feel for babies. Crawling is not easy. My only goal was to reach the quad and get in. After what felt like both a moment and an eternity I reached the top of the hill and could see that Wish was there, waiting at the quad. She looked at me with mournful eyes as if to say "I'm sorry, that pretty much sucked for both of us." Moving was agonizing but I managed to hunch up to the wheel and start it. I lined her up next to the quad, took her reins and led her to the gate. I unsaddled her from the quad, thinking how much I hated to let my saddle drop to the ground. Crazy thoughts, but there. I put her away in a blur, fueled by fear and adrenaline. Even now, from the emotional distance time brings, I'm so grateful that my decision to move myself didn't result in making my injury worse. I don't know what things would have looked like if I had stayed put as night fell, but I do know that I put myself in serious jeopardy by choosing can-do and by moving.

In addition to activating my can-do genes, my accident also triggered expression of a hyper-polite gene in me. My grandmother grew up during the depression and she was huge on manners, thank you notes, and never arriving anywhere empty handed. That goes deep in me too. The guys in the ambulance were very kind, and were probably way ahead on me on the true severity of my accident and the journey I would soon be facing. I'd never been in an ambulance before and because of the shock cocktail I was on it felt like a very awkward social situation. We introduced ourselves and they got to work. They asked if I would like something for the pain and I replied politely "No thank you." They told me very nicely that whether I wanted something for pain or not, they needed to place an IV as a matter of procedure. I have a high pain threshold which could be a sign of either toughness or idiocy, but I also have high anxiety about any kind of IV situation. When I realized the IV was not a choice, the paramedic asked if I would let his intern insert the IV. This triggered an immense politeness crisis. Having worked with animals and knowing how to set up an IV myself, I know from experience that it is, if not an art, at the very least a fine skill. Coupled with my anxiety about IV's being anywhere in my vicinity, this was a problem. Politeness won out as we were all being so nice and nobody wants to be the one jerk in the group, so I agreed. He concentrated and I closed my eyes. His first try went south and we both looked like we might cry. "Another try?" they asked nicely. I said very nicely "No thank you." Things were beginning to feel real.

Surreal is when the emergency room doors open and everyone is on high alert and you realize that it's you who's been elevated to top priority. It was a very clear sign of the seriousness they'd been alerted to expect but I was still clinging to "I won't feel very good tomorrow" looping through my head. My husband Pat sat at my side in our cubicle as we waited for the results of the battery of tests. One hour, another, almost three hours passed as we held hands and waited. Separated only by thin curtains between cubicles, you cannot help but hear the stories of others as they await and are given the news that has the power to change their lives irrevocably.
The ER is thick with black Sharpie lines.

We were silent witnesses to the conversation next door as an elderly gentleman diagnosed with a heart attack was flown out on a Reach helicopter. We quietly said a prayer for him as we waited for our own news. As his brother and wife left, they told my husband that they too had been listening to what we were facing, and they were pulling for us. Months later we met when they recognized me as I was running errands in town and introduced themselves. They told me they were struck by how polite I was in the midst of it all. Life in a small town is full of sweet moments like these. Somehow, while my future hung in limbo, politeness felt like something normal and non-accident I could hold onto and gave me some semblance of control in moments which were very quickly spiraling out of control. Fueled by the adrenaline cocktail buzzing in my veins, I held on to all I could to keep the fear from settling into my heart.

Waiting for test results takes on a life of its own, as you balance between two realities – what used to be and what could be. The quiet of our little cubicle was broken when the ER doctor came running in and yelled "Your back is broken, put your legs flat, now! Put her back on the board!" A team hit our room like a flood as they prepared to send me to a trauma center. The weather had changed and flying out on the helicopter was no longer an option so they prepared an ambulance to take me on the long ride over the hill. Reality shifted like a reflection in a broken mirror and we knew nothing would ever be the same.

My own black Sharpie line; forever dividing the old me from the new, broken me. Pat and I held each other's eyes as we sought to process what had just been said. He held my hand tighter as if to say "I've got you." I held his hand like a life-line until they rushed me out to the waiting ambulance to begin the trip over the hills to the trauma center.

I was whisked into the ambulance and into the dark night. I felt more alone than I had ever imagined possible. The blood in my veins had turned to ice and I could feel the cold burn through my body as if my blood had just been transfused with antifreeze. We set off into the dark and into my unknown.

Chapter Three

Just Breathe

Keep your mind in the middle.
Trent Loos

I was in ICU five days, waiting for surgery to repair what we then knew to be my imploded first lumbar or L1 vertebrae which had disintegrated upon impact. Turns out that was the loud "pop" I heard when I hit the ground. For a biologist you'd think I would be smarter than I am and that pop should have told me something big had happened. It should have shut down my instinct to crawl home, but I've learned that shock operates under its own orders.

I used to love the word "implode" and used it as often as possible, but that was before part of me actually imploded. Little did I know it would ever come to have a personal meaning to me and that part of my own body would do the very thing done to has-been casinos which get blown to dust to make room for new casinos. I'd never really thought of imploding and me in the same sentence before my L1 was blown to bits. I didn't even know such a thing was possible. Medically speaking it's called a burst fracture. Pat diligently researched the surgery I needed and possible surgeons. He found one who would essentially need to be a rock star of neurosurgery to perform a lumbar corpectomy, one of the most complicated of back surgeries. He likes to know how things work, so he found a reenactment on the Internet and showed it to my visitors. I couldn't bear to watch. I was in batten down the hatches mode; I battened down and prepared for the storm. I didn't allow myself to examine the harsh reality of the complexity of the surgery waiting for me. Just hearing the details made me nauseous. The neurosurgeon was chosen and the date set: five days out.

Crawling had really not been an option, as tests had shown my spinal cord was impinged upon to 50% by my broken vertebrae. The job of our vertebrae is to give structure and support to the spinal cord, and mine was essentially acting like a poised dagger to the integrity of my spinal cord. The slightest tear could have irreversibly damaged my spinal cord. As it was, we did not yet know whether I would suffer any paralysis. Five days was a long time to wonder who I would be when this was over. The L1 is pretty much the middleman of your vertebrae. The lumbar vertebrae are the big stocky guys of the vertebrae, responsible for supporting most of our body's weight. In my mind, late at night and waiting for surgery, I kept visualizing that my L1 had turned to dust effectively splitting me into halves. It was terrifying wondering if my divided parts would actually stay together the rest of my life. To put me back together would require removing one of my ribs and using it as the basis for a bone graft in a titanium bone cage which would be placed in the gap where my L1 used to be. Fuse it all together, and I would be held together by titanium.

I struggled to reconcile the fact that a significant portion of my spine would be comprised of titanium, chemical element number 22 on the Periodic Table. Titanium: Stronger and lighter than steel. This would take some getting used to. Years later I am still acutely aware that it's inside of me; the titanium bone cage and plates and pins holding me together, which I now call my "hardware." Sometimes the knowledge that I am held together by hardware scares the snot out of me. I've been training myself to love my hardware, because without the technology and audacity that ever caused someone to try out such a complicated fix, I'd be screwed. Now I'm actually screwed together, but in a good way.

Getting through this accident was requiring every shred of grit, perseverance, but mostly faith, that I had. I knew I couldn't do this on my own, I knew that my faith would have to lead and I would have to follow. Every time my thoughts would run sideways I would remind myself of an old western saying my friend Trent Loos told me when he phoned right after hearing of my accident. "Keep your mind in the middle." I couldn't do anything by my own power other than accept what had happened and pray for wisdom, courage, and patience. I knew I was being lifted in prayer by so many people, and I could feel it. I focused on those words and tried to keep my mind in the middle and not off to the bookends of panic or despair.

"Are you breathing?"

The nurses came in hourly and asked. They made it sound like a job, and it was. No, I wasn't. My body was broken and fragile. My spirit felt crushed. I felt part pain, part panic, part everything. My chest felt tight and my lungs were barely expanding to take the deep breaths that would have proved beneficial, both physically and emotionally.

Breathe.

It sounds easy, but we tend to ignore our breathing as it's facilitated by our body's autonomic nervous system (ANS) which takes care of business without our help. Our ANS is housed in the brain and regulated by the hypothalamus and controls much, among them our respiratory and cardiac systems. I've been fortunate enough in my pursuit of horsemanship to take part in clinics of Mark Rashid, a fine horseman and a friend. If you're struggling to grasp something he often asks (it's probably already pretty obvious to him what the answer is) "Are you breathing?" In return I've asked him "You mean I need to ride and breathe at the same time?" It seems the most obvious thing in the world, as without taking in oxygen, we die in a matter of minutes. But at the heart of his question is "Are you truly breathing?" Are you are taking deep, restorative breaths from your core or is your breathing shallow and almost non-existent – a manner of breathing we resort to when we're anxious or afraid. When we are scared our bodies tend to revert to what's called fight or flight mode. Shallow breathing is part of our body's response to anxiety and fear, counterproductive though that is. Focused breathing is a central tenant to many practices of martial arts, meditation, yoga, and birthing classes. Mark's seemingly simple question always pushes my reset button and before I even realize it, my horse relaxes and moves out softly from underneath my formerly clenched-up self. With the "simple" act of focused breathing we move from where we were stuck because my shallow breathing had caused my body to become tight and constricting. Just like magic, when I breathe, my mare breathes and we move easily forward. Just breathe. Mark's a smart guy.

Breathe. The nurses ask again.

Never had I been more desperate to answer Mark's question. The nurse chastised my shallow breaths and asked "Are you using your spirometer faithfully?" I loved my nurses but first of all I had no idea what a spirometer was and second, I hadn't been given one yet. A spirometer, or peak-flow meter, is a device designed to measure timed expired and inspired volumes. This gives a measure of how efficiently and quickly the lungs are emptied and filled. She promptly gave me a spirometer to help my lungs stay expanding while bedridden. The danger of your lungs not expanding while bedridden is that it increases the likelihood of ending up with pneumonia. Not only is pneumonia debilitating at the least and fatal at the most, it would delay my long-awaited surgery date even more and my white-knuckle grip on sanity was already pretty shaky.

I've taught biology to college students and in our study of physiology we learn about the respiratory system. The human lung is an amazing thing, a remarkable structure and vital to a healthy life. The resting volume or total lung capacity of the average healthy male is close to six liters and that of the average female slightly less than five liters. That volume is never completely dispelled from the lungs and only a fraction of that total moves out with each breath. This fraction, ranging from about 500-600 milliliters, is called the tidal volume of the lungs. It's lovely to think of that tidal volume like an actual tide, the interface between two environments as when ocean water and fresh water mix. What this means is that there is always a mixture of fresh and stale (oxygenated and deoxygenated) air in the lungs. Half a liter. That's not so much to bring oxygen into your lungs to keep your body at peak function. That small volume exchanged each breath illustrates how shallow breathing can quickly compromise your body's ability to perform vital physiological tasks. Each time I tried to expel a deep breath the pain was excruciating and my efforts were weak no matter how hard I tried. Even more depressing was my pitiful effort to keep the little balls of the spirometer in the air long enough to pass the nurses' five-second test. Pat had his eye on the thing and I could tell he was longing to use it. He easily reached their mark of success and I was struck again how incapacitated I really was.

Breathe.

It sounds easy. Yes Mark, yes nurse, I wanted to breathe. Deeply and affirming, but I couldn't make it happen. My literal legs had been knocked out from under me and what was left was pain coupled with panic. For a person who'd always joked about being claustrophobic in a ski jacket, it was now a huge issue for me. I couldn't stand to have my feet covered, couldn't stand to have the door closed, couldn't stand the stifling feeling of oppression that snuck up so heavily at night. When the visits of the day were over I felt painfully alone and broken and so very vulnerable.

I was scared.

Chapter Four
Red Jell-O

As you make your way through life, let this ever be your goal,
keep your eye upon the doughnut and not upon the hole.
The Optimist's Creed

Everyone knows a work week can pass pretty slowly, and five days of waiting for my surgery felt like eternity. It had felt like I'd been in a cocoon of suspended reality that had begun when I found myself in mid-air prior to crashing to the ground. It sounds strange, even to me, but the time I spent suspended felt much longer than it could possibly have been, and we all know that gravity is a force you can't argue with.

I had felt what I can only call figurative giant hands scoop under me and I'd felt a yellow light around me. Maybe it was the fading light of day, but the whole experience felt out of this world, literally. It sounds weird, I know that. But somehow a salve of calm and peace had covered me since my diagnosis and had seen me through the interminable waiting, waiting for surgery and my future. *In all things* kept running through my head. Somehow my natural impatience was replaced with a peace that I knew was not of my own making. This peace allowed me to have a calmness the ICU nurses remarked upon daily.

ICU is a pretty wild place. They see some pretty rough stuff in ICU. They see it all and do it all for a 12 hour shift. Some funny stuff happens in ICU, and some incredibly tragic stuff happens and still, they do it all. The ICU nurses were my new best friends. I wasn't doing much as I wasn't allowed to move by myself and it was almost like my room became an oasis of calm for them to drop by in a rare quiet moment. We talked about life and their jobs and the polish on my toes, which a nurse correctly identified as OPI's You Don't Know Jacques. My sisters-in-law Katie and Amy had been taking turns staying with me and we were all impressed that she nailed it. You Don't Know Jacques is the kind of color that looks like someone took all the colors of finger paints and smooshed them together. I treasured the unexpected gift that left me open being able to just listen when they had some small moments of calm in their crazy shifts. It was definitely a God thing, not a me thing, and a bright spot in a dark time.

I loved my nurses. I was entirely dependent on them for everything and they made it easy to be vulnerable through their kindness and professionalism, but most of all, their humanity. I have such great appreciation for all those who cared for me and will be eternally grateful for their help during that time. But the clear-liquids-only diet they had me on? Hadn't anyone in ICU heard of the healing power of steak? I'm not a big meat eater like Pat or my dad, but not being able to eat real food was turning me into a ravenous carnivore. The ICU protocol was to keep me healthy and ready for surgery and as part of that, I was on a clear-liquids-only diet. There are only so many things that make up the category of clear fluids. My friends asked, but they don't serve vodka in the hospital. Plain tea, broth, Seven Up. Thank Heaven for Seven. The saving grace was that liquids included Jell-O.

I hadn't eaten Jell-O for a really, really long time. I learned that it's kind of like riding a bike, you never forget. Red Jell-O. My favorite: so bright and cheerful and jiggly. Sweet nostalgia and chemicals jumbled together in a tiny plastic cup. Red Dye #40 and sugar mixed together bring memories of childhood rushing back through your taste buds with the first spoonful. Oh how I looked forward to that little daily cup of Jell-O. It was almost embarrassing. There wasn't much else to do as I couldn't move, so waiting for Jell-O time filled the space. Funny how Red Dye #40 tastes so good when you have nothing else to look forward to except a sponge bath, fingers crossed that Nurse Tom wasn't on duty. That little plastic cup of red Jell-O was a joyful moment in a long day of waiting.

The goal I'd set for myself, to be an exemplary patient, was a lesson in patience, and Lord knows I had ample opportunities to work that out every day. I was actually doing okay with the waiting and the liquid diet, but some things would honestly try the patience of a saint; and though I'd gone to Catholic school for a while, I am far from saintly. Funny it's the small things that finally broke the camel's back. Jell-O wasn't much in the bigger picture but it was helping me get through the days. I'd come to believe that the only Jell-O served in the hospital was red as it was my favorite and it just made sense. Who really eats the other colors anyway? Then, one day, yellow Jell-O arrived on my meal tray. Yellow? Oh hell no. Those little plastic cups already look suspiciously like urine sample cups. Does anyone really eat yellow Jell-O in the hospital? I have to doubt it. I was being a good patient, never buzzing for help or extra drugs. I was hanging on by a thread; somebody please, please, bring me some red Jell-O STAT. I call BS on yellow Jell-0.

Chapter Five

Dreams

*Let a joy keep you. Reach out your hands
and take it when it runs by.*
Carl Sandburg

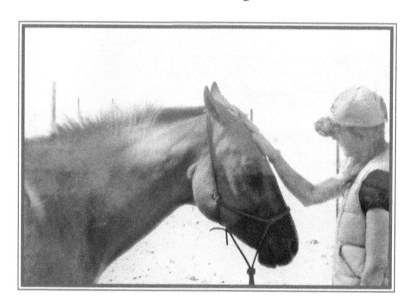

Home coming was full of adjustments. I was wedded
to wearing a brace for three months and to using a walker. My
restrictions were many, which equated to needing help for the
smallest of things. The effort involved in rolling over just to stand
was excruciating. I knew I had to take it a day at a time, but it was
hard not to look anxiously into my new future, which felt full of
unknowns. Most of my time was spent lying down which added up
to too much time to think. Pat and I picked out some movies; movie

watching seemed harmless. I love westerns, and if Sam Elliot or Tom Selleck is in it, it's as good as it gets. We chose a western we'd never seen before, and as soon as it began I realized it was a major mistake. The galloping started right away and so did my tears. Gallons of tears started pouring out, without an off switch. I'd only cried once from the time I'd hit the ground; through the terrifying days waiting in ICU; the nine and a half hour surgery; and a week filled with grueling daily physical therapy the likes of which my therapist said had made San Francisco 49'ers players cry. No tears. Not one. And now, there were enough tears to fill a little bucket. Pat tried to stop the tears, but a switch had been flipped and my emotional wound was ragged and raw. I didn't see the movie; I saw riding I was sure I would never do again. I had just begun to understand the depth of my physical trauma, and this was my first clue to the emotional trauma residing barely under the surface.

Days were challenging but sleep was even more so; if I dreamt at all, my dreams were restless and disjointed. We nick-named my hospital bed the mini-me; the mini-me was my constant reminder that everything was different now. But one wonderful dream stands out. I felt the joy lingering upon waking. In my dream I am riding a dun horse and we are galloping into the sunset. Full-on galloping; moving as fast as you can go kind of galloping. We are in the desert or grasslands, I can't tell from my dream. The ground is smooth and no gopher holes or rabbits or anything spooks this horse. We are flying across the open space, with nothing to slow us down. My mind seemed to be processing my new reality through the western, but unlike my waking life which was now full of uncertainty; in my dream my dun horse and I are fearless.

Thank heaven for horse friends who've always seemed to have had a few hard knocks themselves, with horses and with life. It's hard to have spent much time riding or being around large animals without a mishap or two. My friend Laura came to visit as soon as I was home from the hospital. She was my riding partner and she felt awful about not being out with me the day of my accident. I told her about the movie and the tears which had snuck up unbidden. She's a can-do girl and pretty stoic like most of the can-do women I know. "I'll never haul ass on a horse again" I told her, my voice thick with emotion. She quietly processed this. After a pause she said gently, "But how often do we really?" She said she could remember galloping maybe all of three times in her whole life. She's a solid rider and a great woman all the way around, someone whose opinion and observations I trust totally. Her reality check stopped me mid-crisis. I had to ask myself the same question.

How often did I ride like that? Other than the day of my accident, the last time I can actually remember traveling at a true gallop was well over twenty years ago. My friend Wilbur and I had been practicing polo. After practice we decided to race and made a bet to see who would win and tore off down the side of the field. Polo is a fast sport and polo ponies are used to travelling fast, so these horses knew what they were doing and didn't need any encouragement to fly. I can still feel that day, one of those golden-warm late afternoons where it's hard to imagine that warm air and the sun could ever feel better than they do; the smell of warm sweaty horses and sunshine and the sense of flying, of all feet in the air like Eadweard Muybridge's "Sallie Gardner at a Gallop" 1878 photographic experiment. I remember how intoxicating it was to test the limits of my self and my seat, and to let the horse just fly. No daylight between me and the saddle. Me and my horse moving at full speed; mind, hands, and seat working together to encourage rather than impede speed. Pure and undiluted joy. Wilbur won; but that's okay.

Disclaimer: I was never any good at it but Wilbur's a nationally ranked player, and he's as natural on a horse as anyone I've ever seen.

We like to go fast on horses. Or at least we think we do. Sometimes when we ride and ask for an upward transition we think we're saying "Let's go faster" but often we put up braces that block that forward from happening. We're most often unaware that we are even doing it. Often it's from fear of getting what we're asking for – going faster, or going really fast. Fear was now part of my equation and it had never been there before. Through my dream I seemed to be processing that I would probably never have the option of moving that fast again. But the truth remains, and I thank Laura for it; hauling ass isn't the way I've often traveled or plan on traveling in my riding.

The more I thought about my dream, and I had plenty of time to think, I realized that my dream horse wasn't scared of speed either. I recognize now that Wish is uncomfortable with speed. She wasn't confident enough in herself or with me to be comfortable with speed normally, and especially not the day of our wreck when her mind had left me and I'd ignored it because I had my own agenda: I wanted to get home, and fast. Throw a rabbit into the mix, and under those uncertain and fast hooves and it was obvious why no good came from that combination. Wish's fear of speed was something I needed to address, and I don't think I'd realized that until the dream. Being with your horse moment by moment rather than attached to your own agenda is critical to good horsemanship and as I'd just realized the hard way, to your own safety. Not listening to my horse when I knew better allowed the rabbit to create a perfect storm of an accident because I'd ignored the gap in my communication with Wish, and hers with me. She had let me know she needed help, and I had ignored it.

There's no end point to horsemanship. Horsemanship is a life-long goal. To be great, or even good at it, takes a commitment to be open to continually learning. The truly great horsemen and women never arrive at an endpoint; they continue seeking more enhanced communication with the horses they work with. There are so many layers of finesse in horsemanship that sometimes it feels overwhelming to pursue it, like you'll never achieve even a fraction of their knowledge along a journey like that. I've learned you have to be okay with that and recognize any progress is a win. Good horsemen pay close attention to the movement of each foot, and can tell each beat of all the gaits. They can direct each foot and know where the feet are at all times. The walk is a four-beat movement, the trot a two, the canter a three, the gallop a four. They recognize that working with the movement and placement of the feet allows the rider to be balanced and to create a rhythm with the horse rather than creating more braces and disconnect between horse and rider. In legendary horseman Ray Hunt's classic book *Think Harmony with Horses*, he describes a trot as "He should roll right out in a trot. The life should come up in him smooth…Be part of him, roll with him." Reading that gives me goosebumps as I can see that trot in my mind and feel it. A great horseman can make a walk look like ballet, and the faster gaits look like pure magic. Watching Manolo Mendez work with a horse in hand or Harry Whitney ride and you're seeing true beauty unfold. Great horsemen and women are artists. Watching people of their caliber work with a horse expands your mind to see what a difference that level of knowledge makes for both horse and rider. It's a challenge to seek out true horsemanship, but a privilege to create such a relationship with an animal as incredible as the horse.

Horsemanship requires honesty for it to really work and not just become an exercise. Sometimes that pursuit has big and small bumps along the way. Wish was like many of the horse friends I have, she'd had a lot of hard knocks herself. Wish was part of a big horse rescue case up north of us and part of the collateral damage of a Quarter Horse breeder gone awry. Over fifty horses were taken in the seizure and most were malnourished at the least, and starving at the most. It was an abuse case of staggering proportions and it took way too long for the horses to be relinquished into caring hands. I adopted her and we began our relationship together. I don't know the rest of her story and never will. The challenging thing about horses and especially rescues is not getting stuck on their past. It's easy to envision scenarios for a horse and to tip-toe when working with them because it's easy for us as humans and caring people to overlay our own feelings about what they experienced on to them. What horses need from us is the same, regardless of their past. They seek clarity and consistency, in their herds and with the people who seek to cross the communication divide between human and horse. Some of the best horsemen and women I've had the privilege of watching have observed horse behavior intently for years and they can see what the horse is seeking and provide it in a way the horse understands. They don't get hung up on the story, they get busy with what's in front of them now and provide clarity the horse can relate to and off they go, into a productive and positive future, regardless of their past, both horse and human.

I'd been guilty of tip-toeing around Wish. She's real sensitive and has a personality kind of like an onion. Horses recognize the most minute body language and tip-toeing isn't something they're keen on. As all prey animals must be in the wild, they're constantly on the watch for any threats in their environment and a tip-toeing human no doubt reeks of sneaky. Working with an unsure horse when you're unsure too doesn't help the situation. Unsure horses are already struggling, with fear and possibly physical issues and pain. Wish, like every other horse, was looking to see if I could provide clear direction to bridge our conversation without being too big or too small about it. Most horses are grateful to turn their fear over to a person who shows them the way as clearly and as softly as possible. In the gold-standard book of horsemanship *True Unity*, Tom Dorrance put it "The rider needs to recognize the horse's need for self-preservation in mind, body, and the third factor spirit.......he needs to realize how the person's approach can assure the horse that he can have his self-preservation and still respond to what the person is asking him to do."

I had so much to think about, and now, so much time to think. From the perspective of the mini-me and from hind-sight I could see clearly that Wish wasn't comfortable with a lot of things.

Part of that I had to own because I hadn't filled in those gaps for her. Part of it may just be Wish. Not all horses are the same by any measure. I'm not sure she'll ever be as brave as I might want her to be, but we're not at the end of our trail together yet so I don't know. The encouraging thing is that the horse in my dream was a dun and so is Wish. I'll always remember the times I flew like they do in westerns, and that's okay. Maybe we didn't need to actually gallop into the sunset to be successful together. Maybe a nice, moving out walk heading somewhere with a quiet and calm mind is just as good an end result. My dream gave me insight into a place for us both to head.

It's really amazing what a horse will do for you if he understands what you want. And it's also quite amazing what he'll do to you if he doesn't.
Bill Dorrance

Chapter Six

Chicken Wings, or Why I Love Horses

In the game of life it's a good idea to have a few early losses, which relieves
you of the pressure of trying to maintain an undefeated season.
Bill Vaughan

Women and horses. They go together like feet and shoes, or
chips and guacamole. "The outside of a horse is good for the inside of
a man" has been attributed to many people from Winston Churchill
to Ronald Reagan, and whoever said it was right on, but I think it's
even more true for women. Women tend to be people-pleasers and
sometimes we have to remind ourselves that it's okay to do what
pleases us as well. I have found that for me, horses have helped in
that quest, as I've experienced in my own journey through adulthood

and upon becoming a wife and mother. When I became an at-home mom, I felt compelled to work 24/7 to meet the needs and wants of my family. Somehow I felt that my contribution needed to be non-stop otherwise it wouldn't be of equal value to my former paycheck. With my tendency towards compulsive responsibility, that was a bad combination. Unfortunately for me and probably those around me, it took a serious case of burn-out to realize I needed to pursue things that uplifted me, in addition to my new roles as a mom and wife. My release from burn-out came from rekindling my life's abiding passion for horses. My friends Kitty and Ernie had taken me in back when I was single and horseless and graciously invited me to their place almost every week for ropings and taught me to rope. When years later I recognized that I needed to reconnect with that passion, they opened the door to that world again and sold me one of their rope horses; loaded up the family and Lickety Split in the truck and delivered him right to my door. Thanks to them, I had a horse of my own again and my real journey to horsemanship began.

Disclaimer: My roping skills are slim, notwithstanding Ernie's great teaching and their whole family's mad skills, but I never did rope my horse, and I still have my thumb which is good enough for me.

Why are women so drawn to horses? That's a great question to ask horse lovers over margaritas. My friends and I have had many great conversations about our abiding love for the horse. Some surveys estimate that 75% of riders are female. Historically men were the ones riding and working horses, in war and as transport, but those tides have turned. My love of horses has been with me ever since I can remember. Breyer horses were my love over Barbie's. My friends and I still talk about our Breyer horse collections. My first real live horse was an ancient strawberry roan mare named Pepper; she was someone else's throw-away horse but a five-year old girl's dream come true. I still love roans the best. As a little bitty girl, I'd ride her bareback through the walnut orchards and we would stay out as long as my mom would let me. We gave Pepper a new home and Pepper in turn gave me her friendship and my freedom. I loved that worn-out horse. She was everything to me and I found joy in her velvet nose and a home in her breath. I'm not five any more but their effect on me is still just as powerful.

Horses' identity as herd animals creates an astonishing sensitivity to other members of the herd as evidenced in their behavior toward each other. It's their shared instinct to be hyper-cognizant of their surroundings: as prey animals they have to be, their lives depend upon it. We could take a lesson from horses on being as aware of our surroundings and as mindful of the moment. In the wild it's the stallion that claims a herd and determines where the herd moves, but it isn't the stallion who maintains herd unity. A boss or lead mare oversees the behavior of the group. The lead mare's job is to keep disputes to a minimum and to ensure the daily activities of the herd proceed with as little agitation as possible. The evolutionary soundness of this is that unnecessary agitation uses energy, and nature seeks to reserve energy as resources in the wild are generally limiting. It is the horse's status as a prey species that is at the essence of their behavior. Horse behavior is so incredibly fine-tuned that we denser species often fail to see the incredibly nuanced aspects of their amazing communication. We often forget the deeply-set nature of the horse in our interactions with them. This is really at the heart of much of our disconnect when working with horses – we miss so much if we don't educate ourselves to learn more about the way horses communicate.

As humans we often know from unfortunate personal experience that not all leaders are equal and not all bosses are good bosses. With horses, a good lead mare is a benevolent leader, neither overly aggressive nor overly submissive. Watching a benevolent leader in action (horse or human) I am struck by the confidence exuded in that quietness, not to be confused with meekness. A good lead mare knows when to be gentle, when to go big. The signals she sends are clear as day. It's under her steady influence the herd can thrive. The young learn how to behave from the guidance of the mares and though as foals their youthful shenanigans are tolerated, proper behavior is expected and enforced as they get older. Observe a group of horses to be illuminated. Their dominance hierarchy is clear. If it isn't at first evident who's who in the lineup, it quickly becomes obvious at feeding time. The dominant horses feed first and the others fall into line in order of their rank right behind the leader. You can learn a lot from horses if you open your eyes and your mind and soak it all in.

As I began to study horsemanship I stopped reading how-to books about parenting. The wisdom I was gathering from working with horses, in letting your "yes be a yes and your no a no" was powerful. The honesty of horses and dogs draws me to them like dirt seems to be inexorably drawn to white pants. Horses hold up a mirror for us to see ourselves clearly, if we're brave enough to look at our reflection. Without saying a word they offer the opportunity to join into that clarity of communication with them. They offer, and it's up to us to take them up on it.

One of my struggles with raising my boys was realizing that their children's honesty wasn't always appreciated in undiluted measure. Not many people appreciate being called "the woman with the moustache" or "that old bald man" and though it pained me to put a lid on them I realized it was my civic duty to reduce if not the number, at least the volume, of their overly observant comments. It was a challenge to foster the truth which resides in children while moderating it to the barest extent I could for social mores. My boys came up with some real good ones, and some of my favorite conversations ever have been with them and their unvarnished observations about life.

Kids, as well as horses, keep us honest. I appreciate the importance of choosing your words carefully so as not to hurt others but sometimes there's a fine line between truth and BS. Sometimes as grown-ups we need reminders of that. My son Jake has retained that transparent honesty and his wisdom well exceeds his years. Some of the wisest and sanest things I've heard have come from his young mouth; he reminds me of Yoda, only taller, and not green. I admire that honesty in him and have no worries because while his honesty is powerful, he has one of the most compassionate hearts I've ever known.

There is no fine line between truth and BS with horses. To enter into communication with them in an honest way you need to be able to meet that honesty with your own. Often at the beginning of a clinic the riders are asked "What do you want to work on with your horse?" It's a telling question. Often what comes out is a tale of a rider's relationship with her horse and it can feel like we're taking a field trip to a therapist's couch. Buck Brannaman is one of the greatest horsemen alive today and a strong advocate for rider responsibility. He's said, "A lot of the times rather than helping people with horse problems, I'm helping horses with people problems." If you've watched him, you'll know what I mean. He's adamant about telling people what they need to hear, which isn't always easy, but he says what needs to be said for the rider's sake and especially for the horses'. Buck says "The horse is so honest. They live in the moment. And what they do, whether they need to protect themselves or whether they need to accept you is really directly relative to how you make them feel." It's not always easy to acknowledge the baggage we bring with us to the party. I'm grateful to my horses for pardoning my sloppy attempts to communicate with them and for giving me the eyes to see the unnecessary baggage I've been carrying and to learn how to set it down and move on.

After reconnecting with horses after so many years away, I felt like I'd come home. I knew little about actual horsemanship, but I felt grounded in their presence like I hadn't in a long time. The time spent with them filled up all the spots that had been drained in my efforts to be all things to all people. Sometimes I had felt like the girl in Rumpelstiltskin, trying to spin straw into gold, and failing miserably. I'd grown up just figuring out riding on my own, and now that I was beginning my journey into true horsemanship, I realized how little I actually knew. That realization could end in intimidation when I was working with horses on my own and my confidence in my own ability would often disintegrate. Those sessions often ended in confusion and frustration for me and my horses. My uncertainty translated to them and began a spiral of bad communication. Grown-up me was afraid to make a mistake, to do anything less than perfectly, whereas kid-me just rode.

Mark Rashid once told me "Does it really matter if you do something wrong? People ask me all the time in clinics why I use this halter over that one or do this rather than that....... But does it really matter? Try it again and see if that works. Try another way. As long as nobody gets hurt, what's the harm?" Hearing someone of his talent say that was powerful. I've taken that lesson and run with it. The first time I was ground driving a horse a helpful observer told me that my arms were moving around so much that they looked like chicken wings. Needless to say, ground driving became the last thing on my mind and my chicken wings moved to the front of my brain. Having an audience can add another level of insecurity, but there will always be somebody with something to say. Talking with my female horse friends I've realized that we can be pretty hard on ourselves, with horses and with life. I've found that there's an unspoken question in the air when entering into a partnership with a horse: can you turn off the external noise and cut yourself loose from those expectations you put on yourself and those that others have of you and just be present. No past, no future, just right here, right now. I've finally learned that in working with horses you need to let what's said outside the round pen stay outside and focus on being present with your horse. I've learned to pick carefully whom I want to be learning from and working with, as evidenced by their horsemanship as well as their personal integrity with themselves and those they mentor. I'm a few years older now so it just doesn't bother me as much anymore.

Thanks to Mark's observations on mistakes, I can look back on chicken wings with the added wisdom of his insight. So what if my arms looked like chicken wings when I was ground driving? With practice and the confidence that comes from integrating Mark's observation that more than likely any mistake I make isn't going to scar anyone, there's an incredible liberation. Making mistakes can set you free.

Chicken wings never killed anybody.

Chapter Seven

Embrace the Schlub

I base most of my fashion sense on what doesn't itch.
Gilda Radner

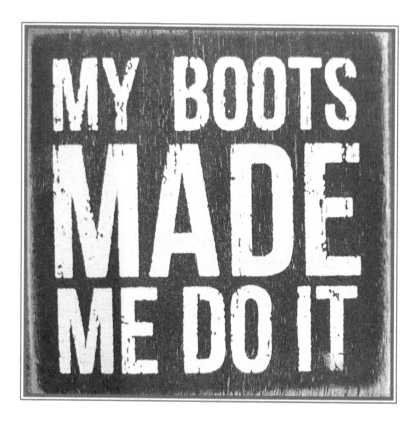

Boots and jeans used to be my go-to outfit, but in the aftermath of my accident and out of necessity my daily outfit had become a pair of slip-on slippers and sweat pants. It's not a good look. There were really only so many things that went with the clamshell brace I had to wear for three months and sweatpants had become a staple. Boots were impossible to put on so in addition to re-thinking jeans, I'd also had to re-think footwear. I missed my boots. I missed my jeans. I'd fallen far down the scale of cute outfits. Now I was relegated to wearing slip-on slippers, the kind that make a scuffling sound if you don't consciously focus on picking up your feet and setting them down again carefully. Picking up my feet was still a challenge so I was shuffling around the house making that scuffling sound which was annoying as nails on chalkboard and driving my own self nuts. It's hard to feel encouraged while wearing elastic waist pants and noisy slippers. Sometimes it's the small things that wear you down, and I was feeling pretty down.

My friend Crissi McDonald called to check up on me. She asked how I was doing and I told her the truth. I'd been trying really hard to maintain a positive outlook and attitude but petty as it sounded, it was really wearing on me to feel like such a sloppy schmuck 24/7. I told her that I'd spent most of the day watching every prison show I could find on the National Geographic channel. What an eye opener. You never want to wind up in a Peruvian jail. Trust me. She'd called while I was midway through the episode where an Australian teacher had tried to smuggle 10 kilos of heroin into Thailand in a suitcase he had actually checked through security. I was learning a lot watching National Geographic. Crissi laughed and told me that she had a secret life which might make me feel better. Turns out she was addicted: addicted to Netflix, the show "Bones" in particular. She had started from episode one, season one and she was now up to season five. She was spending hours every day working through Bones. She highly recommended I join her. Each season has 22 episodes at 44 minutes an episode, so we did the math and calculated that ought to at least get me most of the way through my last month of wearing my brace. Our math only worked if I watched a minimum of six hours of Bones a day. I didn't have anything else to do, so it seemed like a good plan. She said that Bones had great characters and the show was clever and dark, just how she likes it. I laughed and told her how her choice of binge-watching material was so much better than other choices she could have made, like Jersey Shores for example. To Crissi's credit she didn't even know what that was.

"What about all the stuff I could be doing or should be doing?" I asked her. Somehow I'd thought I would spend my recovery doing something productive and instead I found myself discouraged and schlepping around my house in sweatpants. Crissi is a wise woman: a Philosophy major and a naturopath, a wonderful horsewoman, and pretty freaking funny to top it off. She cleared her throat and I waited expectantly for her deep philosophical thoughts. "Embrace the schlub," she said. Huh? "Yea," she said again, "Embrace the schlub. There's a time for everything. I just spent three years traveling non-stop with Mark (her husband Mark Rashid), working, training, teaching, and now I'm tired. Its winter here in Colorado and everything that needs doing is done, so I'm watching Bones for now and its okay." I let her point sink in. Sometimes it just takes the time it takes, and there are times for going fast and times where you have to be okay with going slow. This was a lesson I needed to learn. We thought Embrace the Schlub would make a good t-shirt and or bumper sticker, and though we might be the only two who would buy one, that would be okay. The first motto she'd dubbed me with while I was still drugged up in the hospital was Drugs on Board. Considering where I'd started this journey, Embrace the Schlub was definitely a sign of my recovery progress.

It was difficult processing what recovery should look like, or even if there was a should. Surgeons focus on surgery and not post-surgical progress, so navigating my way through the recovery process was sometimes confusing and often lonely. I was learning things about myself, good and bad. I realized that I have a very forward-moving energy, and that I am not very good at being still. Even at the end of yoga, the savasana part, I'm making a to-do list in my head.

Most of my accidents have been broken bones, but nothing close
to this. Recovery felt like limbo. I wasn't hanging on to mobility
by a thread anymore and my neurosurgeon said I was recuperating
well and at a timely pace but I only saw him to review my monthly
X-rays which he would say looked great and off we'd go until the next
month. I struggled with unrealistic expectations of wanting more
from myself; thinking that a positive mind set and good physical
condition to start would somehow catapult me to an accelerated
recovery. I had never experienced physical trauma like this before and
I overestimated how much I could achieve with just my own grit.

    I know I'm not alone in dealing with the aftermath of an
accident. If you haven't experienced how much trauma takes out of
you, it's easy to underestimate how much it impacts your body, mind,
and your soul. Conquering my mind was sometimes harder than
fighting through my body's recovery. My body was responding to its
own healing, but my mind was frustrated by the seeming slowness
of my progress of every day, but most of all by the uncertainty of
how I would be when recovery was actually over. My impatience
and frustration were quickly followed by guilt because I knew how
fortunate I was compared to so many others. I can walk. Not
everyone who walks away from a wreck can say the same. Many of
those I shared hospital quarters with didn't receive such good news
and will never be able to walk. I am blessed. I am blessed and I
remind myself, I am blessed beyond measure.

    Crissi's wise counsel to embrace the schlub helped me
realize that, yes, there is a season for everything. Some of them just
aren't even close to what we'd envisioned for our lives. But it is in
reconciling our vision with our reality the challenge lies. We inhabit
space with almost seven billion other travelers, all of us residing
temporarily on a planet in constant rotation and orbit, and things
happen. Good things, bad things, horrific things, and incredible
things. It's in those things that aren't the things we planned that lie
our challenge. Smuggling heroin in a suitcase is a really bad idea; I

gave myself points for not having that on the list of dumb things I've ever done but I had my own wreck to process.

The words "in all things" had been placed on my heart and now I was learning what that actually meant. I was finding my way through the wreckage and learning that the physical process was only a tiny bit of the healing I needed. I saw clearly that there was a choice in front of me: I had to choose to adjust and point toward the sun and gird up for whatever life throws and find my way forward. Thanks to wise friends I was learning that sometimes that means you've got to just embrace your inner schlub. It takes the time it takes. And thanks to my smart friend Crissi and my own Netflix subscription, I had something to look forward to. That, and to burning my slippers when I was done with them.

Chapter Eight

Good Things Come in
Small Packages

*Dogs feel very strongly that they should always go with
you in the car, in case the need should arise for them
to bark violently at nothing right in your ear.*
Dave Barry

Horses share my affection with dogs. I've also apparently
hit my dog limit which, I'm told, is three. The sign on our gate
says "Caution – old dog, young dog, several stupid dogs." It's not
completely accurate as we meant not to insult our dog trio but to

convey that we're not a house to be messed with. What it should really say is "big dog, medium dog, and little dog." I still can't believe we have a little dog. I spent most of my life being unflaggingly biased against little dogs. When I had considered going to vet school I told my friends that a good name for a clinic would be "Big Dogs Only" or something like that, just to make it clear to little dogs that they weren't welcome. Little did I know how vitally important a little dog would become to me.

All of my opinions and biases about little dogs disappeared when we got Scout. My boys wanted a little dog and I finally conceded. I figured that a dog was a much better Christmas gift than Black Ops for PS3. I knew that caring for a dog would be much better for their development than killing zombies. Pat, while he likes dogs, wouldn't be classified as a dog lover. His idea of a good dog is one that sleeps outside. After the stellar sales pitch I gave to convince him, it was a done deal that it would be me waking up every two hours to take out the teeny tiny half Jack Russell, half Yorkie pup the boys named Scout during what turned out to be a very cold winter. A bladder the size of a dime required lots of tending.

Loving animals and especially dogs as much as I do, it was ridiculous of me not to have realized that I would quickly bond with him and grow to love him in spite of his little dog size. Scout's size was remarkable. We kept waiting and waiting for him to grow – nothing. He inched his way from tiny to a little less tiny to very small. We waited some more, thinking that maybe he would hit a growth spurt. Not only did he not get any bigger but he began to sprout unruly hair in every direction instead. And my gosh, what big ears he had. It was as if all that growth that wasn't invested in growing his body went into his ears. His ears had a life of their own. They were like his very own antennae system. You could tell his mood from his ears. They did things I've never seen ears do before. Before long we were all enthralled with his tiny yet potent terrier'ness. In spite of all of my life-long resolve, I'd fallen head over heels with a little, little dog.

Scout doesn't know that he's a little dog. He's also my first terrier and I learned fairly quickly that no matter the size of the terrier, in his mind he's all that and more. Scout functions in the absolute certainty that if he isn't uber-vigilant, all hell will break loose around here. We have a big dog and a medium dog too, but in Scout's mind they are apparently slackers. He wakes each day with a mission to patrol the perimeter and he's so good, he deserves a medal. The awesome flip side of this attention to safety is that he also loves to snuggle. He has a very good grasp on when to patrol and when to chill. He knows the routine of each day and goes through the day with me. Every morning I took my boys to school and Scout would go too. When we got back home he would go with me to feed the horses. He went out with me each evening to feed. He knows the daily drill and thrives on it. He barks at the deer on our property whether they're there or not. He barked at the kids at school whether he'd seen them four years in a row or not. He barks at all of us when we come home, just in case I guess. Scout's take on Shakespeare would be "To bark or not to bark; that's a stupid question." His philosophy on life may well be "I bark, therefore I am."

I'd never imagined that saying yes to this tiny terrier would result in him galloping into my heart and staking out such a huge territory there; not only would he become my lodestone, but he would come to reside at the epicenter of my healing.

Chapter Nine

Damn it, Costco

Part of the secret of success in life is to eat what
you like and let the food fight it out inside.
Mark Twain

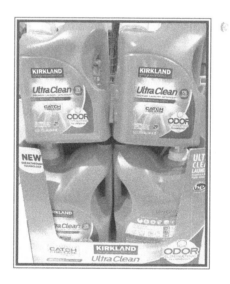

My friend Trish hails from Alabama, and it's thanks to her I
know that the saying "Bless your heart" is really southern code for
"not so smart." Well-intentioned, but not so smart. I'd been saying
that quite a bit lately after my accident and I meant it in only the best
way. Bless Pat's heart; he'd done so much for me and for our family
after my crash and burn. He took the boys to school, picked them
up, did the laundry, and shopped. All of his efforts were amazing,
but it was the shopping that was interesting. Only 25% percent of
the people in our family would be heart-broken if they never saw

a vegetable again, and that person was me. The other 75% were whooping it up as I wasn't in charge of grocery shopping anymore. The last vegetable I'd seen was a wrinkled carrot that had gotten lost in the vegetable drawer. The vegetable abandonment got even worse when the three of them discovered the joy of shopping at Costco without me.

Our closest Costco is an hour and a half away. I very rarely get to go into Costco because it's far away and to be honest; it scares the crap out of me to go alone. We have very limited shopping options near us so the wonderland of delightful options in Costco overwhelms me. My mind goes blank when faced with all those choices and in that blankness I panic and buy soap. I enter through the vast doorway with good intentions and emerge hours later hauling a trailer full of things I didn't know we needed until I saw them, including cases of Irish Spring soap. The last time I bought soap Pat said he hoped he lived long enough to use it all. I was in the hospital when my three guys discovered the joy of their first solo trip to Costco (close to the hospital) and discovered a playground of indulgent shopping without me there to mess it up.

Costco has a wondrous produce section. It sparkles with every kind of fruit and vegetable you can imagine. Beyond being drawn to their book section, the produce section calls me personally by name. But I wasn't there to intervene. No way were tomatoes, potatoes, and asparagus ending up in their man-cart. Cases of Corona, beef jerky, Air Heads, Otter Pops, and peanut butter pretzels took their place. A vegetable would have quailed in fear just looking at all the tasty competition that took up residence in our pantry. Case upon case of Top Ramen, teriyaki noodles, and macaroni and cheese filled the shelves. I was afraid to open the door. But you know what? I couldn't be more grateful to my husband for all he did during those months I was laid up. If that gratitude needed to include massive doses of Top Ramen, so be it.

Sometimes love hurts, but it's worth it.

Chapter Ten

Kissing Bug

Accidents will happen.
SpongeBob Square Pants

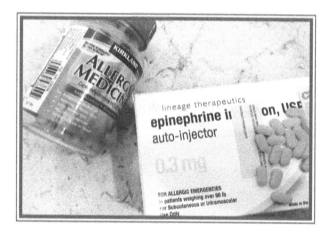

Our family is kind of ridiculous. We've been blessed with good health but when we fall, we fall hard. Three of the four members of our family ended up in the emergency room the week of my accident. 75% of us. Pat ended up in the same ER the day after my accident. We'd spent all night the night before in one hospital emergency room and then in the trauma center of another hospital from 6:30 p.m. until 5:30 a.m. That very next night he ended up back at the same ER with a severe allergic reaction to a kissing bug bite. Kissing bug is the common name for the assassin bug subfamily Triatominae. Kissing bugs are very common in the southwest, and Middle and South America where they are often vectors of Chagas disease, or Trypanosomiasis. They may be called kissing bugs but they're more like assassins to our family.

Kissing bugs are attracted to the carbon dioxide emitted when we exhale. Sleeping people are often bitten since they're easy targets. Kissing bugs are blood-suckers like the mosquito. Allergic responses to their bite range from mild irritation to anaphylactic shock. Pat's reaction is more near anaphylactic. ER time. Being the thrifty guy he is, he waited as long as he could in the hospital parking lot (prior to succumbing to anaphylactic shock) before checking into the ER. Sometimes thrifty can go too far. This wasn't our first rodeo with the kissing bug. The first time he was bitten he immediately developed a rash and his throat began to swell as we rushed to the hospital. Fortunately I have my M.D. from WebMD and I'd guessed that he'd been bitten by a kissing bug and gave him several Benadryls on our way out to the hospital. They rushed him to ER where he was immediately hooked up to intravenous steroids to knock down the rapidly escalating allergic response. Now he travels everywhere with an Epi-Pen. The ER staff knows our family pretty well now. They knew us even better three days later when our son Jake ended up in the ER with a broken finger. Our insurance carrier must have been wondering what the hell was going on. Years of nothing, then three ER visits in one week. Our recurring theme is broken bones and anaphylactic shock.

Prior to breaking my back, my most exciting broken bone story happened during my first week of grad school. We'd gone rock climbing one afternoon and just as we were coming down, I popped off a little boulder and hit my heel just right, causing that unmistakable cold shiver broken bones bring. The heel, or calcaneus bone, is a small cup-shaped bone and when it breaks it's usually not good. My friends carried me down the mountain and promptly set me down on an ant hill. I know intimately where the phrase "ants in your pants" comes from. They then helped me into the car and promptly slammed my hand in the door. That break resulted in eight weeks on crutches for a non-weight bearing break which made the

"School of a Thousand Stairs" a real challenge.

My car and all my worldly possessions had been stolen the week before. We'd gone rock climbing to make some happy memories to make up for the stolen car fiasco.

Life.

Chapter Eleven

Saved by a Five Pound Dog

His ears were often the first thing to catch my tears.
Elizabeth Barrett Browning, about her dog Flush

The evening of my accident I had crawled through our front door and collapsed on the rug in our hall. Scout knew something was wrong. He took the baseball cap I'd been wearing and ran through the house shaking it. He'd been my constant companion from the day we'd brought him home; my tiny side-kick. When the ambulance came and carried me away, it was the last he was to see of me for two weeks. I thought of him all the time and wondered how he was processing my disappearance. Each day in the hospital was an exercise in perseverance. I missed my life and my family dreadfully. And I missed Scout. I would lie awake and wonder how everyone was doing at home without me, including Scout. Sleep is hard to come by in the hospital which seems like a perverse oxymoron. Sleep is healing and hospitals are places of healing, so why is it so hard to sleep in the hospital? It seemed like a cruel joke that every time I actually fell asleep I'd awaken to someone asking me a question or taking some kind of sample. My favorite hospital wake-up was a woman shaking me, asking "Michelle, do you want to go to rehab?" It took me a while to process that one. First I had to wake up and remember where I was, and secondly, I had to ask myself what kind of rehab this stranger thought I needed. Finally I realized that she must be talking about some kind of rehab other than the kind I was thinking she meant.

In the hospital, rehab is code for physical therapy (PT) which I needed before I could be released. Start to finish I was only in the hospital twelve days, not long for the magnitude of my injury, but all I wanted was to be home. I began to appreciate how prisoners are motivated to make parole. I was determined to be a star patient so I too could be scheduled for an early release. The nurses tracked my daily progress by measuring the amount of food I ate, which was then scored with a percentage. It wasn't long before I started to develop some obsessive behavior. I fixated on how they decided to award my percentage. Every percentage counted as improvement, and would speed my release. There wasn't much else to do besides wait for the Jell-O delivery so I began to estimate my own percentages. I took exception to the nurses' measurement if I felt cheated out of a couple percentage points. Can anyone really tell the difference between 35% of a sandwich and 40%? The scientist-me took it seriously. Each evening I was given a menu to check menu options for the following day. In spite of checking the items myself, somehow each day I was surprised by what ended up on my tray. Like hospital life wasn't stressful enough without waking up to a bowl of cold stewed prunes. I couldn't prove it, but it sure seemed like my mom got a hold of these menus somehow, because I know for sure that wasn't me checking the box for prunes. She denies it but it seemed an unlikely coincidence as she fed me the same kind of food (prunes) when she came to help me after I'd been released.

They waste no time in the hospital. I'd been rolled out of surgery at 9:00 p.m. and a physical therapist was at my bedside at 8:00 a.m. the next morning. Walk? I had no warning this was the deal. The sheer physical and mental force it took to roll over onto my side to put my brace on just in preparation to get out of bed was immense. The pain was excruciating and I was spent by the time I'd managed to raise myself to a seated position. But somehow, I was up and standing with the therapist, Pat, and our sons by my side. Tears burned my eyes as I struggled to find the strength somewhere deep inside to force myself to take those steps. They were miniature, but they were steps. I was walking. The therapist cheered me on and told us she'd done PT for some of San Francisco 49ers and that the first step after huge injury often incapacitated even the biggest guys. It helped put into perspective the magnitude of what this would take. My son Max was impressed. He loves sports, especially the 49ers. I was less impressed because I know the fortitude of women. If she'd told me that an offensive lineman had a drug-free delivery, then the playing field would really be level.

It was her job to get me started until I was assigned a therapist of my own. Starr. Contrary to what you're thinking, Starr wasn't an exotic dancer. Starr was a tall, muscular, athletic kind of guy and funny as hell. He wasn't easy on me, but his manner and humor helped balance the pain. I was determined to exceed all of his expectations so that he'd fast-track me to be released. He said I was a bit of an overachiever. I'm one of those people who feel they should study for their annual eye exam. Starr was right. I was all about over-achieving my way out of rehab. More than anything I wanted to be home. I wanted to be away from the timelessness of the hospital. I wanted to touch my family. I wanted to sleep in my own house. I wanted to see Scout.

On day thirteen, that day came. I sobbed as the hot water from my first shower in thirteen days flowed over my head. No shower had ever felt as good. It was the only time I had allowed myself to loosen the grip on my emotions I'd held so tightly to avoid losing it completely. My tears mingled with the water as the kind assistant who was showering with me let me stay in as long as I wanted. I was going home. Terrified, but going home. I begged Pat to bring Scout with him to pick me up. Scout hadn't seen me in almost two weeks. He didn't know what to make of the new me who was wearing a hard armor rather than the soft jacket he was used to. He lost his traction on my clam-shell brace and looked at me as if I'd been abducted and returned worse for wear. He finally settled in on my lap on a soft blanket and we began the long drive home. The long drive home was filled with twists and turns, but I was overcome with relief to have my five-pound dog on my lap. This wasn't the only long and winding road I'd be on as now the next road to recovery had begun.

My relief at being home with my family (and Scout) was overpowering. Scout must have felt the same way because he set up his command station on the mini-me hospital bed I slept in. He was at my side 24/7. I could feel his eyes on me like tiny brown laser beams following me if I got up even for a moment. If I went into the bathroom, he went into the bathroom too and sat on the bath mat watching me. Usually the bathroom has some degree of privacy but he didn't care. Dogs aren't shy. His devotion to keeping an eye on me was okay with me, as being in the hospital pretty much strips any semblance of personal modesty from you as there's no such thing as private parts in the hospital. Sponge baths from Nurse Tom had seen to that.

We finally set up a little water bowl for Scout next to the mini-me as it dawned on me that he hadn't left my side even for a moment for food or water. He went from being the world's most active five pound dog to the world's smallest couch potato in nothing flat. I wasn't going anywhere, so he wasn't going anywhere. He would roust himself when the home-health nurses came and stand on the bed to better keep an eye on them. Recovering from the surgery and anesthesia had pretty much knocked me out, so I slept a lot. So, Scout slept a lot too. Nights in the hospital had been the worst. Sleep is evasive so it's difficult to find sleep's peaceful release. I'll never forget the comforting feel of Scout's five pounds settling on my blankets as the sleep that my battered body craved finally overcame me.

For two weeks I had held onto my emotions with an iron grasp. I'd been afraid to let go because I felt pretty certain that if my tears started they might never stop. With Scout I didn't have to explain what had happened. I didn't have to fight the emotion in my voice when people asked me how I was. He was just there. Five pounds might not seem like much dog, but his utter devotion and uncomplicated love emanating from his tiny frame helped my real healing begin.

Chapter Twelve

Hotwire

There are three kinds of men. The one that learns by reading. The few who learn by observation. The rest of them have to pee on the electric fence for themselves.
Will Rogers

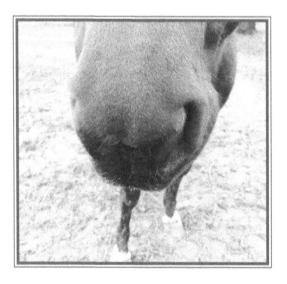

My respect for the electric fence began pretty early.

Electric fence, or hotwire as it's often called, is a common means of fencing for partitioning sections of land. My respect for the wire came from relying upon my dad to tell me whether the fence was hot or not. We were moving cows between pastures. I asked him "Was it hot?" He said it was not. I took his word for it because he is my dad, and thanks to his confident reply, I grabbed the wire as balance as I worked my way through the fence. A second later I was stuck in the middle of the fence holding tight to the wire. It's surprising how your hand gets stuck grasping the wire while the rest of your body is at a 90 degree angle trying to shoot out of the way. It was what you'd call a teaching moment, in which I learned two things. One, always think of the fence as hot unless you've turned it off yourself and two, my dad is probably right 50% of the time. Touch a hot fence with wet hands and you gain a whole new appreciation for the miracle of electricity.

There's an old country saying about cattle and the electric fence. Somehow they always seem to know when it's off. How they do this is a mystery but it's fairly common knowledge in the country. It could be that each day they hold an election and some cow gets nominated to be the fence tester and the winner keeps at it all day until the next election, when they can pass the baton to the next fence tester. Eventually the fence will be turned off, whether by intent or by default of the fence keeper. It's at that exact moment that all cattle in the vicinity head over to the fence and have their way with it. This is no big deal if you have light-weight animals with good manners, but if you don't, they could wind up just about anywhere like marbles. And they usually do.

I'm not taking cheap shots at cows; I've been a fence tester plenty myself. It's usually ended up with me in some kind of trouble, but sometimes it's kind of like wiggling a loose tooth, almost irresistible. Part of fence testing is human nature, but that doesn't necessarily mean it's a good thing. Horses seem to have a healthier respect for the hot wire than most of the cattle I've known, but they test the fence too. Many mornings I've gone out to feed and instead of seeing everyone lined up waiting for me, I've found six horse butts sticking out of the barn, hay all over the place. The chubbiest horses always seem to be the ones who are out most often. Most of the time they don't even have the decency to look sheepish. Hoot in particular seemed to be the official fence tester. If there was any kind of disconnect in the fence, he would find it. He could find big gaps and tiny nooks and crannies. He'd end up on the other side of the fence when I couldn't find anything out of place leaving me wondering how the heck he did actually end up on the other side. I still don't know as I never found the opening of his last escape. I think it's possible he actually rolled under the fence, to our mutual surprise.

The hotwire itself can't keep a determined herd in; it's intended to serve as a signal giving a heads up that the boundary is something to be respected. Sometimes we're not even thinking about testing the fence but we end up on the wrong side of it anyway. There was a rash of accidents right after my own. My sweet friend Jeannie was bucked off her reliable old mare during a horse camping trip and ended up with a fractured T12 and in a back brace. A friend was shot at point-blank range, to the horror of our community. Whether we're testing the fence to look for openings or just minding our own business, sometimes you just end up on a journey you never saw coming. If there's anything I've learned from my accidental journey through the valley of recovery, it's that it's really important to have your resources stocked up.

Our paths lie through both mountains and valleys. We live in a world where loss is as normal as joy, and walks through a valley come. Journeys through our valleys are harder if we're traveling on fumes. Many of my college friends were hard-core ski mountaineers, and they were always prepared, down to the smallest detail. Their survival on those treks depended on being ready for the journey. You can't aspire to climb big mountains without being prepared for an avalanche. My own time spent in the mountains taught me that having the right tools for harsh conditions made the conditions much less harsh and much less dangerous. I was way, way down in the valley now and I was learning how important it was to keep my soul-engine from running on fumes.

Sometimes it feels like a one-ton boulder of awful fell across your path and that there's no way around it. There's no way to move it alone, unless you happen to be a heavy equipment operator. This journey was teaching me to look at that immovable boulder as 2000 lbs. of rocks instead. Moving that first 1 lb. rock of pain may take all the energy you've got for that day. But tomorrow there will be one pound less to move. That may be the day you move two or three rocks out of the way. Some days you just can't move any, and that's okay too. Recovery has days of huge gain and many more where it seems there's absolutely none. And so it goes until that the pile of rocks is so small that you can actually keep moving, through the pain, out of that valley. Taking that first step after surgery felt like it might just kill me. But the next day I was able to walk half way down the hall. It's easy to feel overcome and heavily burdened by the weight of our struggles, and I've found that having a stash of joy (and Cheetos) can help keep you afloat. I've been working on that, to fill up my soul with every joy I can count, especially the small things, as those seem to be the kind sprinkled through our daily lives. Living in wait for those seven days of vacation just doesn't fill up your soul-reservoir.

The Danes seem to have it figured out. Denmark consistently tops the list of the annual World Happiness Report. The Danes have leaned into their months of darkness and cold and they build small comforts or hygge, into their daily lives. Hygge is the small stuff. Spending time with a few beloved friends, a cup of coffee and a piece of chocolate; lots of cake (and bacon) and the Danes have found a way of life where they create small moments of joy in their dark, dark winters. I was in my own dark winter and I was finding too, just like the Danes, that these small comforts were helping me build a life raft when recovery seemed too far away to grasp. I've learned the hard way not to underestimate the cumulative effect of small joys. Small joys may seem too small to make a big difference, but I've found that those small joys were some of my greatest moments of solace when I've felt almost empty.

I'd consider it joy if I could solve the mystery of how Hoot got through the hot wire. Chocolate never hurts either.

Chapter Thirteen
A Serious Case of Horse Envy

A horse! A horse! My kingdom for a horse!
William Shakespeare, King Richard III

Thou shalt not covet is the tenth of the Ten Commandments. The commandments are God's mini reference list of good rules for living, but, man I was coveting big time. I had a serious case of horse envy. Two days running I'd watched someone riding out into the hills behind our property, and the envy was so powerful it just about knocked me over. The winter had been wet and miserable. I wasn't able to ride by any means, but every rider looks forward to the advent of spring when the weather turns and our thoughts turn to heading out to trails and to long rides in the perfect air of spring. The seasons had finally changed and spring had hit powerfully. Overnight the brown dry hills had become a verdant carpet dotted with yellow and purple wildflowers. It's said men are the visual sex; their physical responses and emotions triggered by what they see. If that's true, I must have a Y chromosome. The sight of that horse and rider being trailed by the world's happiest dog crossing through the fields of yellow knocked me to my knees with desire. Coveting, envy, call it whatever, but the emotion it stirred up was anything but tame.

My desire to be that person overwhelmed me. I wanted to be, once again, everything that person represented. Horseback on a spring day, happy dog by your side, is my idea of perfection. Instead, I stood watching from afar, a clumsy voyeur, strapped into my brace and stewing in envy. I did a modified turtle-shell kind of limbo under the fence so I could at least lay my hands on my own horse. My horses had been freaked out around me as my whole energy was off and awkward and insecure. I was off and they knew it. It translated into horse as somewhere between kinda creepy to all out creepy. Fortunately, I'm lucky to be loved by an old horse and Simba came up to me in spite of my weirdness. He's a palomino and when he's half way between shedding out his winter coat and half way not, he looks pretty strange. Getting close to him is like blowing on a dandelion. Clumps of shedding white-blond hair floated up my nose as he stood quietly and let me gingerly wrap my arms around his neck as best I could and bawl. It had been so long since I had had my hands on a horse that his intoxicating, peppery smell was a thousand times more powerful. Few things in the world smell better than a horse on a warm day. Freshly cut grass, alfalfa, babies, lavender, and baking bread all make the best smells in the world list, but a warm horse in sunshine is number one. My tears mixed with his shedding hair, and stuck to my cheeks. Simba stood and let me cry until I was dry, and the tears were a catharsis.

One of the biggest struggles during my recovery was that I was hurt doing something I love so deeply. If I'd been hurt in a car accident it would be traumatic every time I got back in a car, but traveling by car is pretty much a necessity. Riding a horse isn't. It is one of my dearest pleasures, but it's not a necessity. I don't make my living at it. People who love horses often spend a lot of money not making a living at it. The reality that I almost lost my ability to walk due to a riding accident forced me to assess what this love would look like in the future. Plenty of people asked me the question which wasn't really a question: "You're not going to ride anymore, right?" To ride or not to ride, that was my question. I think of my family and my responsibility to them when I make decisions about my pursuits. There may be people who think my choice to ride again is frivolous and possibly even irresponsible, and at the least, nuts. But Pat and I talked about it, and talked about if I would and if I should. I have answered it with "I want to ride." For me, the best view on earth is the view you see from between a horse's ears. I just couldn't imagine a life without being on horseback or working with horses again, some-how. I just had no idea of how to get from where I was to back in the saddle.

Shannon came to visit a few months after my wreck. It was so good to be in her presence. Her energy and empathy are healing. She's been an Army helicopter pilot and a healer in one lifetime. She offered to do craniosacral adjustments on some of my horses. I sat in the barn in a dusty chair and watched her work. It was a gift to be in the barn that day, watching what she does and watching the horses respond. She worked on Sundance and Simba and then Wish. When she was done she asked me if I wanted to just sit on Wish for a minute. How much I wanted to surprised me. Wish stood quietly and Shannon helped me get on. Emotion welled up so quickly and unexpectedly, I had to get off and get a hold of myself. That little sit on Wish's back was overwhelming. I got back on and took the feeling in, and got back off. I thanked Shannon and Wish and got down, with a jumble of feelings. Wish was my emotional lightening rod. I realized she wouldn't be my come back ride.

That wave of emotion made me wonder if I could ever get back on without falling completely apart.

Chapter Fourteen

Hay Fever

Hay is for horses.
Michelle Scully

My husband has hay fever.

Hay fever is a bad deal and not to be confused with spring fever, which is a good thing. Pat has anywhere from a mild to moderate allergic reaction to hay. People sometimes say hay fever, but what they're really talking about is a generic term for any kind of an allergic reaction. The fact that Pat has the real-deal hay fever dawned on me one morning as I was in the barn loading up the feed cart with hay. What had been a twice daily chore had been relegated to my husband

and sons Max and Jake for over four months as I was unable to walk to the barn and not allowed to lift anything heavier than a toothpick. Four months later, on the anniversary of my crash and burn, I was able to do my own chores once again. It felt incredible. Funny how the most mundane aspects of our lives are the things we hunger for when the regularity of our daily lives gets blown apart.

I'd craved my daily chores while I was in the hospital, doubting whether I'd even be able to do them again and trying not to freak out with the uncertainty. I enjoy feeding time. It's an opportunity to get outside, walk with the dogs, and check everything out. The dogs think going off to feed is as good as it gets because they are out sniffing everything, peeing on everything, sneaking horse poop, and being with me. Everything about being outside feels good to a dog. I enjoy the fact that they enjoy it. I love the smell of the hay in the barn; grass and alfalfa hay smell amazing. I hate an empty barn, because it means the hay hose has run down to a drizzle and the hassles of finding and paying for decent hay is once again on my to-do list.

As a farmer's daughter, I appreciate hay. As a horse owner, I have an even stronger appreciation for good hay. My parents farmed alfalfa and even though they've retired from farming it's still kind of a family tradition to be full of opinions about it. Our dinner table conversations often revolved around past hay harvests and shared recollections about good years and bad years and how rain always seems to come mid-July right after you'd mowed. If hay isn't a part of your daily life it just sounds weird but to a hay farmer and/or horse owner, hay is great conversation. The search for good hay is like Monty Python's search for the Holy Grail. Good hay makes us happy.

The true beauty of feeding is that the horses are so happy to see you. Horses are designed to graze 24/7 but in the world we've put them that rarely happens. The average horse now only eats when we feed him, which is usually twice a day. You can imagine that if the sole thing you were designed for, to graze almost without ceasing, wasn't an option, watching someone haul hay to your vicinity would be pretty close to the best thing that had happened all day. And if you're carrying a bucket, you're greeted like someone bringing the Publishers Clearing House winnings to the front door. All horses love a bucket. The bringer of hay brings happiness. I had missed that. Simba, who never forgets that he was once starving, nickers to me and I swear he almost licks his lips. Monty, the retired Arab endurance horse, whinnies and practically crawls under the fence with his long giraffe legs to help me. Pat's horse Sundance practically dances on tiptoe because he's wondering what took me so long this morning; they like to eat early but I am moving slowly yet. Hoot, the Missouri Foxtrotter, dances along the fence line, full of personality as always. Luke the giant Mustang pins his ears and let's everyone know that he's first to eat, just like he does every day. Nothing's changed except me. Wish waits a bit in the back, but knows that she's going to get her fair share. Wish used to be first in line, but both of us have changed since our accident together. I'm not the only one processing our wreck.

Feeding time is a great time to make sure everyone's feeling okay. It's amazing how quickly an injury can spring up out of nowhere. Looking them over for cuts, a foot favored, standing back from the herd; all are signals that something's not right. It's better to avert a crisis before it starts, if you can. After one lesson learned the hard way, I've made a practice of checking digital or "distal" pulses to check for early signs of laminitis which may be triggered by carbohydrate overload if the spring grass is too abundant. Feeding is a very important part of the day and I've missed that. I breathe in the scent of the horses which resets my compass for the day and makes my soul happy. On this special day, I silently tell them how happy I am to see them again, just as I remember. I tell them it's not just seeing them, but more importantly being with them again in our daily routine. I thank them for what they bring to my life and my gratitude that that part of my life is not over.

Spring has arrived and the horses are starting to look great. Everybody looked pretty shabby when I saw them last in late January; the winter was wet and the mud endless. Anyone who has horses knows how mud can just wear you out. It's amazing what spring weather does for a horse. Everybody radiates shine, except Simba who has kept his furry white winter coat in the middle of his body only. His front and rear ends are shiny blond palomino, but his midsection looks like an albino caterpillar gone wild. I have missed so much and I am trying to catch up. It would be a dream to spend the afternoon cleaning everybody up but it's too soon. I'm chomping at the bit to do everything, right now, but I will bide my time. Everything is beautiful. Even the pile of horse poop circled perfectly by tiny yellow flowers that look like miniature stars is worthy of a picture.

Who needs a calendar; I can measure the passing of time by the amount of hay in the barn. The barn was full of hay when I had my accident. When I was finally able to go down to the barn for the first time about mid-March, it was just about empty. If you're used to the ebb and flow of the hay hose, you can appreciate how much time has passed by how much hay the hay hose has shot out of the barn. The hay hose is essentially a measure of money – a full barn equals a good dip in your checking account. A dribbling hay hose means you need to fill it up again with a good shot of money. Thanks to my dad, the barn is again brimming with hay: beautiful, grassy, Oregon hay. Although he and my mom are retired from farming, he still is my hay pusher and he keeps me supplied. The smell of well-put up grass hay in the barn makes me dizzy with happiness. There's still so much to do in the barn, as always, but now I am doing it. I am finally down there doing it. Seeing all that hay struck me viscerally. I'd dreamt of the most mundane details of my daily life and promised that whenever I was able to do those things again, I'd relish every detail, and now I was standing in the exact moment I'd been dreaming of.

The thought came to me like a light bulb; my husband has hay fever. I'd been going nuts over being out in the barn with all that beautiful hay and what struck me so powerfully that morning was that Pat has *hay* fever. Hay makes his eyes swell and his skin itch and his nose plug up. But there he'd been, for almost four months, feeding hay to six horses he could really care less about. He'd been wonderful about everything since my accident and surgery. It's really an eye-opener when you go from being a super independent person to being dependent upon the kindness and care of others. It's kind of a double-edged sword. It requires care and kindness on both the giver of the care and the recipient of that care. You need to be okay with accepting help gracefully and the vulnerability that comes with it. Pat stepped up to the plate big time during this whole experience. He took on all the daily comings and goings of our sons and got them everywhere they needed to be. He even shaved my legs for me when they got out of control. He helped me without making me feel frustrated by my own helplessness. I had learned a huge lesson about being vulnerable and being okay with that.

While I look forward to the whole experience of twice-daily feedings, Pat could care less and yet he had done it out of love for me without a word, but with lots of Flonase. He gave his time, risked his sinuses, out of love for me. Our boys were wonderful too, as neither of them cares much about horses, but they cared for me through taking on my horse chores. Fortunately for them, neither of them have hay fever. But my husband just spent almost 120 days with plugged sinuses, hives, and itchy eyes just for me.

My heart swells just writing that.

Chapter Fifteen
Turn, Turn, Turn

To everything there is a season, and a time
to every purpose under the heaven.
Ecclesiastes 3.1 (KJV)

Walking under an ancient oak this morning, I could feel the thrum of the cicadas, their song rising in intensity as I passed by. The sound is crazy-loud but I found it oddly comforting. Each May I know to expect the song of the cicada. Each May their distinctive song announces their presence, without fail. The male cicada's song is unmistakable. For us word geeks, *cicada* stems from the Latin word meaning buzzer, which is a great description. Their remarkable cacophony increases as their numbers grows, drawing a thin line between hypnotic and crazy-making. The first time I heard the cicadas singing, I thought a power line down must have fallen down.

The cicada's fascinating life history has symbolism in many world cultures. The cicada's shell, which the nymphs drop during molt, is used in Chinese medicine. Some cultures regularly eat cicadas; the female is particularly popular because she's meatier. Delicious. But to the less gastronomically adventurous, their song is what's most notable. Their distinctive mating song requires no special entomological talent to identify and is so well recognized it is often used in Japanese movies to symbolize a scene set in summer. It is so loud that it's reported to be capable of causing permanent hearing loss (if for some reason the song occurs just outside of the listener's ear). After mating, females lay their eggs in the bark of a tree. The newborn cicadas hatch and immediately drop from the tree and may burrow up to nine feet into the ground where they remain from two to seventeen years depending upon species. When environmental signals indicate that it's time to begin their mating cycle, the nymphs make their way to the surface where they molt and transform into translucent-winged adults who will mate, complete the life cycle, and, not long after, die.

Despite my own personal struggle to recover, the world had continued to turn to its own perpetual calendar. The cicadas show up in late spring each year and just start doing their thing. Winter, after all its false stops and stutters, had finally given way. The earth had turned to rebirth. After months of being cooped up inside with limited mobility, I rejoiced that winter had finally passed. The earth seemed happy about it too, and my soul was filled with joy to see the spring. Nature is a powerful clock, tuned to a circadian rhythm of life, responding to the changing length of days. As day length gets shorter or longer as the seasons shift, plants and animals detect even the smallest changes in sunlight and temperature and respond. It's always some kind of season around here: the ticks that show up in January like an apocalypse making us jumpy and paranoid; the tiny April frogs I find hiding in my boots; the June "face" flies that drive the horses crazy and defy even fly masks; the weird little blue beetles of July. We tend to be removed from the cycles of nature in our predominately indoor environments. Over the years I've learned to watch the incremental changes in my horses' coats. While it feels to me like we're still in the hot days of summer, the horses know differently. The nights are becoming cooler, and that change is reflected in the thickening of their coats long before I've caught on to what they already knew; fall is in the air. Being inside for so long has made me feel out of sync with nature. It makes me happy to reconnect and realize that although I've been disconnected, nature hasn't missed a beat.

It's cathartic to be outside. There is so much beauty just outside my door. I love all the animals I used to see daily and have missed them all, like the little Black Phoebe who hangs out in our yard and sings a greeting each morning and the tiny Yellow War-blers who descend upon our fountain mere seconds after we start the water up again after a long winter. There's nothing exotic here, only the simple beauty of ordinary little birds following their own daily rhythms. Today walking amidst the cicadas' song, I was struck by the profound constancy of the seasons and all of life that's dependent upon that. Being inside for so long had felt so insular, and being able to walk outside again filled my heart and lifted my soul.

Sometimes I have a perpetual playlist in my head, kind of like the soundtrack to my day depending on what's going on. The song Turn, Turn, Turn made popular by The Byrds kept popping into my head. I don't really like 60's music or that song in particular, but I knew most of the lyrics because they are taken almost entirely from the book of Ecclesiastes in the Bible. The song was a popular anthem against the Vietnam War in the 60's. The thought of a season for dy-ing and healing seemed morose to me when I was young, but I think the song's been in my head now because it suddenly makes sense as I was turning to my own season of healing.

Getting a diagnosis is one thing; accepting it is another. It was instinct to fight against the reality of my broken back. My flesh and brain screamed silently in rebellion against the brokenness of my back. There wasn't one fiber of me that was okay with what had happened. I'd fought against succumbing to daytime anxiety and nighttime panics, wondering if I would ever feel whole again. I had to work each day to accept that this was my new reality and to try to make any progress however I could. One question came to me un-bidden; I didn't like it but it kept bubbling up. Could I accept my brokenness without raging against it? Could I embrace my new reality and believe it was possible to become the better for it? I struggled with this question during the anxious nights where panic would settle on my chest like an elephant. I couldn't even entertain the thought that something could come out of this other than loss and grief over how I had been, and who I had become.

Something about the silence of the night unraveled all the positive energy of the day. During daylight I could focus on other things, but nights were tearing me up. My breathing would become ragged as anxiety overcame me and I would sob quietly while I prayed for some peace. For so long, I could feel progress each day, shooting me forward from incapacitated, to walking, and walking even more. But I'd reached a point where I was stuck, and the question of whether I could come to terms with my new truth was on a loop in my head. This was all new and unfamiliar and I had no frame of reference. In the dark I would try to calm my breathing to keep the panic pushed down. I would pray but many nights I heard only silence. I've always struggled to be quiet enough to hear God's voice speaking to me, and more often than not when I'm trying to hear, I hear the sound of my own voice chiming in to break the silence. But, there have been other times in my life when I've heard so clearly, it's been unmistakable. Some of those times I have listened and other times not; I've followed in Jonah's footsteps more than once and ended up in the proverbial belly of the fish until God's patience won out. One night as the elephant pressed on my chest again, I prayed a tiny, desperate two word prayer. "Help me." In the darkness I heard, "Today you are good." This time I heard clearly. I've heard people say that God speaks to them in full paragraphs, but I'm glad He approaches me with brevity as I can only process four words or less. We spend so much time looking into the past and into the present; it's easy to skip the now. None of us know the number of our days or what they hold and I'd been so focused on worrying about what might be, it was compromising my right now. Peace settled in my heart. Those four words gave me the peace I'd needed. I could breathe. In the nights to come I slept, and the elephant left me alone. Today, I am good. Day at a time, I can do this.

The cicadas' song had filled me with thoughts more eternal

than ephemeral. I'd never expected to get life lessons from an insect. This journey of recovery was filled with unexpected lessons and un-expected teachers. The cicadas reminded me that life is a marathon, not a sprint. Sometimes it takes two years, sometimes seventeen, sometimes you mate and sometimes you die, but to everything, there is a season. Being reminded of the cycles of life helped me to see that healing is as natural a progression of life as every other season. How just like God to know exactly how to speak to me, through nature and all of nature's creatures, which have always had my heart.

To everything - turn, turn, turn
There is a season - turn, turn, turn
And a time for every purpose under heaven

A time to be born, a time to die
A time to plant, a time to reap
A time to kill, a time to heal
A time to laugh, a time to weep

To everything - turn, turn, turn
There is a season - turn, turn, turn
And a time for every purpose under heaven
The Byrds

Chapter Sixteen

Needled

As soon as healing takes place, go out and heal somebody else.
Maya Angelou

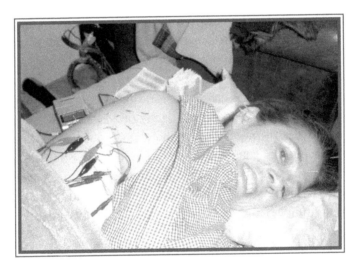

Pain was part of this package, from the first pop announcing that my L1 had burst to the daily pain of recovery. I've already admitted that I have a high tolerance for pain and not too much sense. I'd chosen drug-free deliveries for my two sons. Both turned out to be very difficult deliveries, and in retrospect a few drugs (or a lot) would have been a really good idea. I blame it on my mom. I'm pretty sure I've never seen her take an aspirin. Thanks to her I grew up just toughing through things. I blame my unrealistic expectations of childbirth on her too. My tiny little mother gave birth to me over lunchtime, in twenty minutes. The doctor finished his sandwich and then welcomed me into the world. It's no wonder I misjudged that whole deal.

From the first moments in the ambulance when I'd said "no thank you" to pain meds, I had tried to do the same in the hospital, but people much smarter than I knew that pain needs to be properly managed or it can throw you for a loop. I really wanted to limit my pain meds to the bare minimum when I got home, which was a challenge as the pain of just rolling over to put on my brace before I'd even stood up, was punishing.

Fortunately, within the first week I was home a family friend phoned to check on us. He had just graduated from Five Branches University, a traditional Chinese medicine school, with a fellow student who had just moved to our community. He highly recommended both acupuncture and her. I was game for anything. Needles sounded kind of counterintuitive, but I trusted him and was desperate to try anything which might ease the pain. Kimberly Curtis soon contacted me. When she understood the severity of my accident and my limited mobility, she immediately offered to drive out to our place twice a week to "needle" me. She would come, set up her table, set up her needles and spend close to two hours twice a week needling me. Scout wasn't sure about the whole stranger sticking pins into me concept, so he took up post on the bed to oversee and make sure she wasn't hurting me. Scout and I quickly realized that Kimberly was a blessing.

The surgical entry site, also where my rib had been removed from my left side, was tender and numb. Numbness is a typical side effect of surgery, as the nerves enervating the area can become damaged when the incision is made. There's no doubt in my mind that lopping off a rib is also pretty traumatic to your skeletal system. Each acupuncture treatment helped to reduce the post-surgical pain, and it also decreased the numbness of the area surrounding my scar in measureable amounts. Kimberly and I nicknamed the vast expanse of tingling, numb skin as "The Land of Numbish." We thought about Numbish kind of like the ancient supercontinent Pangea we'd learned about in Geology courses long ago. These are the kind of weird conversations that can happen when two science'y types get together. We hoped that Numbish would get progressively small and smaller, just like Pangea did as it broke apart into smaller continents. Thanks to Kimberly, each week the numb area, which had started out feeling huge and unassailable (like Pangea), became smaller and smaller until it became a much smaller area more the size of a little continent like Australia (or maybe like a medium-sized island like Madagascar, if you're still thinking about plate tectonics).

It was such a relief to feel my body begin to heal. To know that it could. That knowledge took root in my heart like a tiny seedling and gave me hope that there was a way forward. Kimberly tended to my scar and titanium fusion with a healer's hands and a healer's heart. Huge amounts of my pain management and physical recovery were thanks to Kimberly's magic needles. But beyond the acupuncture, she helped me to see that there was a road to recovery and she helped me to find mine. Her confidence in me, that I had the determination to do this, helped me believe when I was shaken and unsure. She walked beside me when that road felt impenetrably dark. We are fortunate, we are blessed, when others walk beside us when we need encouragement, and walk ahead of us to shine a light when all we can see is darkness.

Chapter Seventeen

The Catahoula Way

In case of rapture, grab a dog.
Michelle Scully

Do all dogs seem the same to non-dog lovers? I wonder. I enjoy meeting new dogs almost as much as new people. Sometimes more.

It's hard for me to pass by a dog without asking if it's alright to say hello. It's hard for me to understand how some people just don't care for dogs. Perhaps it's because they think all dogs are equal? Maybe they think all dogs are equally likely to jump up on your nice clothes; equally ready to put their noses in socially unacceptable places; equally unrepentant lickers of their own privates? But if you do appreciate dogs you easily recognize that the cheeky Chihuahua is so very different than the ever-ready Jack Russell Terrier. You know the difference between a Chesapeake Bay retriever and a Chocolate Lab. We dog-lovers know that each breed has its own distinctive personality. Over the years I've come to know a wide spectrum of dog breeds personally and have learned they can be as different as apples are, well, to zucchini. The cliché about apples to oranges just doesn't seem to stress the differences enough.

My first introduction to the Catahoula was while I was eating a tiny $9 bowl of soup in the eponymous Catahoula restaurant in Calistoga. Both Pat and my dad measure the value of food by the quantity. Farmers like value. By neither's measure did the little bowl's value add up to $9. The soup was delicious but I couldn't take my eyes off the photographs decorating the walls; beautiful pictures of dogs with haunting blue eyes and a stare that penetrated your soul. Pat was unmoved and continued trying to make his tiny bowl of soup last but I was entranced. We'd barely gotten home before my research began. I'd had a Dogs of the World poster on my wall as a kid and I'd been proud of being able to name them all without cheating. I'd never seen these dogs before.

Catahoula is said to be Choctaw word meaning "clear water", which I think is just beautiful. The Catahoula, more properly called Catahoula Leopard Dog, was little known outside of Louisiana where they are celebrated as dogs of legend. Louisiana loves the Catahoula Leopard Dog so much they've named it their state dog. Right on, Louisiana! The Catahoula is a working dog, known for its fierceness of character and tenacity. Their tough nature and ability to hunt and herd in the deep swamps endeared them to ranchers who knew that they would always come back with the lost animal they'd gone in after. Strong enough to chase longhorns out of brush and swamp, the Catahoula dog works from the head and not the heel end as most working dogs do. Going head to head with an angry longhorn requires some serious intestinal fortitude, something the Catahoula has in abundance. They've been described as having the spirit of the wolf, speed of the Greyhound, strength of the Mastiff, and the assertiveness of the Beauceron. Mix that together and you get one tough, smart dog that's a trifecta of muscle, brains, and instinct.

Shortly after my obsession began, I just happened to find

a litter of Catahoula pups from Louisiana parents for sale nearby. Anyone who's just happened to come home with a new dog or horse knows how this works. You always hitch up your trailer, just in case. After promising Pat I was just going to look at the pups, I drove home with the littlest one and she became our dog Cassidy. As we got out of the car, the big dogs came running up to say hello. My concern that Cassidy might be scared by their goofy enthusiasm was dispelled when she growled convincingly enough to back them both off. All of six pounds, this was our first clue to her attitude. Cassidy the Catahoula quickly became the boss.

Catahoula's are all instinct. I've always taken my dogs to dog school, but it was a whole new world with a Catahoula. Taking a Catahoula to dog school is kind of like taking a college student back to kindergarten and telling them to try hard to keep up. Cassidy looked at me with disdain as she watched the other dogs flopping around trying to figure out what was going on. Her look said very clearly, "Stay at your heel and follow you and these dopes around the ring? Done." We could have graduated the first day but I felt obligated to get our money's worth. Farmer's daughters like value too. Cassidy learned every command the first time she heard it. Agility was a cake walk. See-saw bridge, tunnel? No problem. Only one thing. Cassidy in the ring versus Cassidy in her native element, outside: two different dogs. Cassidy outside is the Catahoula of instinct. There are scents to follow, squirrels to kill, business to attend to. I quickly learned she had very selective hearing.

All dog breeds have their own thing. Some are water dogs, some won't go near it, some have boundless energy and others are couch potatoes. Some live to play ball and others don't know what to do with one. Playing ball with a happy dog is one of life's simple pleasures. My recovery was challenging for me, but it turned out to be an unexpected boon for our Golden Retriever Kai. I couldn't do much, so much of my day was spent hanging out with the dogs. Kai lives for catching a ball. We played a lot of ball while I was mending. Kai's idea of playing ball is basic: I throw, he fetches, and we do this until he almost dies, so I stop before that happens. It's Ball 101. I throw, he fetches; life is good. Until Cassidy decided that she wanted to play ball too. Retrievers are the experts at fetch; but Catahoula's, not so much.

It turns out playing ball isn't necessarily simple. Kai and I were learning that there are some iterations and Cassidy's was this: I throw the ball, Kai runs after it, Cassidy runs after Kai, Kai returns the ball to me and drops it at my feet. Cassidy steals the ball, runs off with it and drops it in her food bowl. Kai and I found this new-found interest of hers hugely annoying. Kai's forlorn look made me feel sorry for him, so I would retrieve the ball from her food bowl, and Cassidy would actually grin. I'd throw it again and we would try to get our game going in the "right" direction. Cassidy grins, Kai looks perplexed, and again, I fetch the ball. We do it over and over again. I resisted the urge to pick Cassidy up by her spotted tail and swing her over the edge of the hill. Kai and I aren't very smart so we continued to play. After throwing the ball about 350 times, I tell Kai "Last one!" and look forward to washing the gallons of dog slobber off my hands. You know it's time to quit when you throw the soaking wet ball and dog saliva lands on your nose. Last throw. Cassidy, who'd taken a break from her version of playing ball, suddenly leaps up, steals the ball on Kai's last return, and off she goes. Kai looks so crest-fallen I just can't leave him hanging, so off I go to fetch the ball once again. Cassidy grins and it begins again.

I hate to admit how slow I am sometimes, but it's obvious I am, so there. I admit it. After about the eighth time of this new ver-sion of Play Ball, it slowly dawned on me that Cassidy was enjoying playing ball just about as much as Kai does, if not more, measuring from the smirky look on her face. Who decided how playing ball is supposed to go anyhow? It had seemed reasonable that someone throws, someone returns, but to a Catahoula perhaps playing ball is really an entirely different exercise; an exercise in confounding and thwarting. Maybe it's her interpretation of The Art of War. Cassidy looks just as joyful after a rousing game of her version as Kai does playing his. Once this took root in my head, I began to see that while Kai and I hate her version, she's playing her own way and she's having a great time. Goldens enjoy the classic "throw-return-drop-slobber-do it a thousand more times." The Catahoula concept seems to be more psychological than physical. A kind of complicated version you could call "confound–dominate-smirk." Light bulb moment. Playing ball obviously isn't the same to everyone. I guess I should accept her Montessori approach just as much as I accept Kai's .After all, she had quite successfully trained me to play her way.

Just when I think I'm figuring this all out, Scout decided to join in and play his own terrier version. I throw, Kai fetches, Scout chases Kai, Cassidy steals the ball, I fetch it, and we all start over. One night as we were doing our Three Stooges version, I watched 90 lb. Kai being chased by 50 lb. Cassidy and 5 lb. Scout. Scout threw his own tweak on the game and went from chasing to stealing. He was ecstatic when he got his little peanut-sized mouth around the slobbery tennis ball and ran off with it. He was drunk with his new-found power and refused to drop it. Watching the three different breeds of dogs play this crazy game, I had a vision of birth-order. Cassidy, the eldest child who decides how things should be; Scout, the baby without any limit; and Kai, the happy to get along middle child who just wants to play ball, dammit. The bottom-line is that all three of them are having fun, whether it made sense to me or not. I came into this with my own notion of playing ball, but I've left realizing that fun is in the eye of the beholder, or the dog breed.

Maybe I needed to look at my own situation with new eyes too. Again, I was learning more from the dogs than they were from me.

Chapter Eighteen
Rabbits, Rabbits, Rabbits

*Confront your fears, list them, get to know them, and only
then will you be able to put them aside and move ahead.*
Jerry Gillies

Rabbits seemed to be following me. Maybe I hadn't noticed
how ubiquitous they were before my accident, but suddenly they were
everywhere. I was used to seeing them in my biology lecture telling
the cautionary tale of their introduction to (and subsequent overtak-
ing of) Australia. Now, though, they were popping up everywhere.
There was a beautiful rabbit finial hiding atop a lamp in an article
I was reading in Vanity Fair. Chocolate rabbits were everywhere in
April waiting to be jammed into Easter baskets, but really. Seriously.

Every direction I turned a rabbit lurked, waiting for me. It was possible I was working up a conspiracy where there wasn't one, but it made me wonder. Was this a cosmic clue? Was the universe throwing rabbits in my face on purpose? Could I embrace the rabbit as I did the schlub and forgive the rabbit who crossed our path and set this journey in motion? Could we at least declare a détente? I'd been happier not thinking about that rabbit at all.

I'd finally started driving again. I was still wearing my clamshell brace and was feeling more than a little gun-shy, but I was behind the wheel. I'd been counting the days till I could drive again, but now that I could I found being in a car made me more than a little paranoid. I looked at everyone suspiciously. I probably looked suspicious. Everyone on the road looked like a student driver or a lunatic. Or both. They were probably thinking the same about me (as in, lunatic). Every driver looked like an accident just waiting to happen. I was petrified of being t-boned or rear-ended. I felt like I was strung together with baling wire as if the smallest jolt would pop my screws out like a power screw driver on reverse.

After a few weeks without incident, my paranoia had begun to subside. I'd driven into town to attend a graduation meeting for Jake's class when a rabbit ran out into the road from my left side, in an exact reenactment of the rabbit running through Wish's legs. Instinctively my body (and vehicle) swerved sideways as though to avoid the rabbit. My car lurched across the yellow line, almost in the ditch along the side of the narrow country road. My heart was racing and my body shaking. The only difference this time was that I was in a car, and not on a horse. It felt like the incident had been waiting in my mind, as if my subconscious had been trying to figure out a re-do.

My dad taught me to drive (that's another story). One of the first driving lessons he ever taught me was that you don't swerve for anything. That's part of Country Driving 101. You slow down, but you don't place yourself or those in your car in danger by swerving. I've had a lifetime of conditioning not to swerve. Ground squirrels give you plenty of practice. But this time, when I saw the rabbit shooting across the road, out of the corner of my left eye, just as in our accident, I literally freaked out. I threw myself sideways which was no easy feat in a brace and seatbelt. My body was trembling and I realized that my reaction had come from an unbidden flight response. I hadn't realized that my body had stored the memory and the trauma. My reaction made it undeniably clear that I had more than physical issues to heal.

My lessons seemed to be following me, just like the rabbits.

Chapter Nineteen
Superhighway

I have woven a parachute out of everything broken.
William Stafford

Star thistle is threatening to overrun the superhighway. Yellow star thistle is what it's commonly called; *Centaurea solstitialis* is the scientific name. Star thistle has become lamentably common since its introduction to the United States in the 1800's. It's the poster child for invasive species. Star thistle easily outcompetes native plants, quickly taking over. Science aside, star thistle is uncomfortable as heck for people and horses to walk through. This was my first time walking out on the superhighway since my accident, and I was surprised at how much there was. It had been way too long and being back on the superhighway was an emotional experience. I saw hoof prints which weren't mine, telling me that a neighbor or two borrowed the highway for a ride. The loop around the superhighway is slightly more than a mile, but it might as well have been a million the evening I crawled up the hill so many months ago.

The hoof prints gave me a melancholy feeling, kind of a gut punch reminder that those prints weren't mine and I had no idea when or if they would be again. But the day was too beautiful and that I'm even able to be walking out there dispels whatever melancholy tried to get started. A doe and her twin fawns walking the path keep six anxious eyes on me to make sure I'm not a threat. I'm walking at a good pace because it feels so good to be able to, but I try to bring my energy down in a mini-experiment to see if I can continue to walk toward them and if they will continue to watch without running away. No dice. The mom heads one way and the twins scatter like crazy marbles and run the opposite direction. Why is that? The biologist-me wonders if it's a divide-and- conquer thing; so the mom draws attention off to herself while the tiny twins run for cover. Another guess is that the little bitty guys just don't have any savvy yet because they're practically brand new and they run any which way, just like crazy marbles. Poor mom's got her hands full.

A rafter of wild turkeys (I know this term thanks to the magic of Google, not thanks to seven years of college) runs across the superhighway to get out of my way. Coyote poop is everywhere and it looks like the coyotes have been busy gleaning grapes from the nearby vineyards. Cassidy jogs ahead of me, the white tip of her tail bobbing at one end, the rear end of what's left of a fat ground squirrel hanging from her mouth at the other. She's a happy, happy dog. She was with me when I wrecked and this is her first time back too. Cassidy has her favorite stops on the superhighway. Her routine on the superhighway usually involves killing something, peeing on coyote poop, and a quick dip in the creek if the water's running. A few spots along the superhighway have old dried up leftovers of a dead animal and Cassidy takes a small bite each time we walk by. Whatever it was is practically petrified and it sounds like she's munching on pork rinds. I find it disgusting, but she's happy. She's made a collection of old bones, some of them to munch on later. It's gross, but she seems to like it. Needless to say, I try to keep as far away from her mouth as possible. There's not much that's sanitized about life in the country. Death, as well as life, abounds.

I am so very grateful to even be on the superhighway again, and walking. A little bit shaky, but walking. Not everyone in ICU was so fortunate. That sinks in deep. My gratitude overflows that I am able to walk. *In all things.* I think back to those three small words God had put in my heart way back at the beginning of this unexpected journey. I fast forward ahead to this day, from the vantage point of being able to look back and marvel at how far I've come. Truth told, I wasn't sure this day would ever come. Snips of memory fly through my head, and I stop in the middle of the superhighway to catch my breath as emotion floods over me. There were so many events, big and small, every day in ICU: the peripherally installed central catheter or PICC line, endless blood work, the transfusions, sleeplessness, and the claustrophobia that threatened to overwhelm me at night. I look back and cringe at all the painful things that made up an ordinary day in ICU. Not just my own, but of those in rooms around me.

There were pools of sadness everywhere in the hospital. You couldn't help but know the stories of the others fighting their own battles to survive, almost as intimately as you knew your own. The young woman down the hall whose head injury resulted in her bed covered with netting to keep her from jumping out of it. The stroke victim I shared a room with in rehab, who showed no signs of improvement. The young mother whose legs had been shattered and her three-year old daughter killed when they were hit by a car in the cross walk.

In the cross walk, doing everything right.

Black sharpie lines everywhere; not just my own. Once I'd

felt more or less fearless, but those days were gone. A few weeks saturated with fear and loss will do that. Recounting the actual events of those two weeks in the hospital felt like a vague memory. Looking back I realize that these things utterly did happen, but it's with a twinge of surprise, as somehow it seemed the actual pain was minimized. *In all things.* From the moment I was in the air I'd felt as if I were cupped between His hands. I could feel rather than see a sense of yellow light, and a sense of calmness. The feeling stayed with me through all that followed. I am so grateful for that. Somehow that divine grace gave me the strength to endure by lifting some of the burden of the moment. The words God put upon my heart from the moment I flew up into the fading light of the day shine before my eyes – *in all things.* It reminds me of a song we sing in church which always floods my eyes with tears at the poignancy of it all.

Life.

It's not often what we were thinking it would be, but my heart feels raw and wide open to the uncertainty and the mystery and the blessing of second chances.

Making the trip on foot and reliving the ride that brought me to such an unexpected place makes me wonder if I can recall the exact place where things went so terribly sideways. I try to shut down my whirling thoughts, and just walk. I keep walking, trying to be open to what the path tells me, to try to find where it all went wrong. I remember certain landmarks and in my mind's eye I can see the tree and the manzanita I tried to avoid. My skin starts to tingle and feel chilled as I realize without conscious thought, I've found it. I've found the site of my unfortunate dismount. Cassidy realizes that I'm far behind and circles back to find out why I'm so slow. The memory hits me hard and drops me to my knees and while I cry, my stinky, wet, dead-animal eating dog crawls into my lap. She is all instinct, but not just for finding squirrels. She is very sensitive to her people and I am her person. Her stinky wetness finally calls me back from my memory and I let her go; she runs ahead happily and looks for her next squirrel knowing that she did her job for me. Dogs know when to stay and when to let go.

Now I know that I have found the spot, I try to process how

far it actually was to crawl up the hill. Something inside tells me "crawl" and I get down on my hands and knees. It feels ridiculous but I start. Rocks cut into my hands and I'm conscious of all the sticks and dirt and deer poop on the trail. I challenge myself: Ten feet. Just ten feet. It's awful. Each foot feels like a mile and I'm really glad there's no one out to see me doing this. Finally, the ten feet are behind me. The top of the hill is still far, far away and I cannot possibly imagine continuing this crawl. My jeans are filthy and my hands are embedded with small rocks. It feels again, surreal. I feel eyes on me, and look around to see a raccoon paralleling my path, off the superhighway but perfectly parallel with me. I'm pretty sure that raccoons are primarily nocturnal, but not exclusively, so I rule out rabies. This girl is paying rapt attention to me, and matching my pace.

I can only imagine what she's thinking. I may never know, but I appreciated her encouragement.

Chapter Twenty
Five Months and a Frog

Adopt the pace of nature. Her secret is patience.
Ralph Waldo Emerson

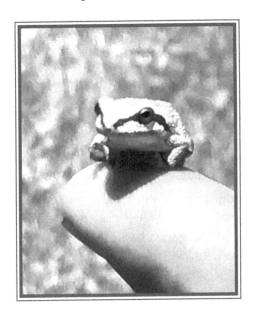

I'd hit the five month mark. Time is a funny thing. It can move so slowly, but at other times it feels as if it's simply disappeared, days falling over the cliff like lemmings. These last five months had moved slowly, probably because slowly was the only way I could move. The summer evening was beautiful, the perfect kind where it's not too hot and not too cold. I'd gone down to hang out with the horses. They were picking at the last remnants of the beautiful grass hay from Langell Valley, Oregon. They grow good hay up there. All six were lined up on a perfect diagonal. Their flanks gleamed in the evening sun, and their tails swished lazily at the last flies still too intent to give up yet for the day. Sorrel, dun, dark bay, chestnut, another sorrel, and palomino. I was working on covering a good part of the color spectrum.

Simba looks like a fuzzy caterpillar. All the other horses had shed out their winter coats long ago, but little tufts of white still clung to him and he looked funky. I'd brought a stiff grooming brush to give him a little touch up before I headed up to the house. It was the first time I'd groomed a horse since my accident and it felt good. Simba let me know that he's got lots of itches he'd like some help with. I got rid of the weird leftover winter hair and down to more serious brushing. Burying my nose in his neck I breathe in his scent, and it's like a whisper, calling me back, reminding me of the depth of that love I feel for the horse. I've tried many times to describe the peppery, sweet scent of a warm horse but I always fall short. He smells like one of the best things ever. If someone made horse smell perfume, I'd wear it.

My attention drifts and he calls it back with a shove of his nose to get my mind back on scratching his itch. His push reminds me that a friendly old horse can knock you over just as well as a younger horse. Gently I remind him and (and me) that we still have personal space boundaries. It was a clarifying moment. Everything has changed for me but his nudge is a reality check. He's the same. He's still a horse and being with horses requires being mindful and fully present. Always. Nothing's changed there. I was grateful for the reminder. I'd doubted I'd ever experience a moment like this again. Something as simple as grooming a horse on a summer evening had seemed impossibly far away. And yet, here I was, five months to the day doing one of the most basic tasks of horse ownership. Something so simple felt anything but. Each brush stroke carried catharsis, a kaleidoscope of memories of times spent with my horses.

The last five months had been a strange calendar. Five days in ICU wondering if I would be able to walk. Four days on the regular floor where my sole goal for the day was to sit up without help to eat my hospital meals. Four days in rehab trying to impress Starr with endless walks up and down the hall to convince him to approve me for early release. Twelve days without a shower. Thirteen days wondering what the rest of my life would be like after major spinal surgery. Day followed day in the mini-me hospital bed at home. Week upon week of wishing I could do the most basic things for my family. I'd have given anything to throw a load of laundry in or to listen to my sons talk with each other on the way to school every morning. Five months had felt like a lifetime. I wasn't even half way to the one year mark my neurosurgeon had said was the magic marker for when my bone graft should be set. Blinders drop from your eyes when the daily life you realize you took for granted is gone. Even ironing was starting to look like fun.

Five months have passed and somehow I'm grooming horses and picking up hay that's scattered all over the barn floor, just like my regular old life. The horses' blankets are around the barn where they've been hanging after being taken off after the long wet winter. I pick up each one to see if it needs washing or repair, finding that it's usually both. I find a beautiful frog looking like a tiny green emerald hiding beneath the first blanket. What would possess this little frog to hide under a dirty horse blanket in a dry barn? He looks up at me, panicked, so I catch him gently and move him to (what I believe looks like) a great frog spot. It's just a little frog, but it hits me big. I'm astounded by the fragility and tenacity of life. Like finding a frog in the most unlikely place, under a dirty horse blanket in a barn. Like taking a hike during a full moon, to the top of a very high mesa on a ranch in New Mexico, only to find a rock encrusted with thousands upon thousands of brilliant red lady bugs, flashing in the light of the moon just like little rubies.

Like crashing and burning on an ordinary Thursday and trying to find your way back, and the slowly dawning realization that you may never go back, but only forward.

Life astounds. And now here in my barn, hides one of my favorite creatures, tucked away like a lover's gift under a dirty horse blanket. I love frogs. My first kiss was stolen over a Maxwell House coffee can. A very progressive boy in my kindergarten class came over to our house and knocked on the front door. He said he had something to show me. I wasn't too savvy at five so I unlocked the screen door and went down the steps to see what he had to show me. "It better be good" I told him when I saw he was holding a coffee can. He tipped the can so I could see inside. It was teeming with tiny frogs, fresh from their tadpole stage and ready to grow. As I looked inside the can, my mouth open in wonder, he shoved it into my hands, stole a kiss, and ran away. As a mother of sons, I'd love to know what story he told his own mom to get out of the house with that can of frogs.

I've always wondered what happened to that boy. No doubt he's made somebody very happy.

Frogs. They're everywhere. For a while I saw rabbits everywhere, but fortunately they seem to have been replaced by frogs, and for that I am grateful. Toads in the front yard, frogs in the back. Frogs on our windows at night, lying in wait for bugs. Frogs hopping across the floors at midnight. Late one night I saw something hopping across the floor, out of my peripheral vision. I grabbed a flashlight and searched around under the couch on my hands and knees. Dust is death to frogs as I know too well from finding petrified frogs stuck in the middle of dust bunnies. I didn't bend too well, but there was no way death by dust bunny was happening on my watch. Half an hour later I was still crawling around shining my light into every corner when I finally found him. The dust had gotten a hold of him and he looked like he was on his last breath. I extricated him from the glob of dust and rinsed him gently under the faucet. I relocated him to the dogs' big water tub outside. He floated weakly on the surface until he got his frog bearings and crawled to the water's edge. I'm pretty sure he said thank you. Another frog saved; hundreds to go.

The next night I found one in the sink. That old saying about how a frog will stay in a pot if it's gradually heated up rather than jumping out? I've always wondered if someone actually tested that one out. I have proof that at least the last part of that saying is true because this frog didn't want any part of the hot water and he was getting out of that sink. I relocated him to the dogs' outside water tub too. All the frogs love the water tub. Every frog who's anyone hangs out in it. They are literally everywhere right now. I was throwing the Frisbee for Kai when I felt something wet smack onto my leg.

I shook my leg, figuring it was a glob of dog slobber but realizing my mistake when I saw a little green frog go flying. I tracked him down and put him in the dogs' water bowl too. He joined his friends and they all looked happy to see him.

It's a full-on frog party in there.

Chapter Twenty-One

My Dog, My Inspiration

In order to really enjoy a dog, one doesn't merely try to train him to be semi human. The point of it is to open oneself to the possibility of becoming partly a dog.
Edward Hoagland

Scout had his own health scare two months before my accident. He usually rides with me to pick the boys up after school, but I had to swing by the store and the day had been pretty warm for October so I'd left him home and hadn't put him in his crate as usual. When Jake and I returned an hour and a half later, Scout was at the front door waiting quietly for us, which should have been my first clue, as he gets so excited when we come home he barks and jumps around like a nut. Jake was the one who spotted Scout's wounded eye, which was swollen and protruding, and we both proceeded to freak out. Immediately I called the vet, grabbed Scout, and drove back to town to get him to the office before it closed for the weekend.

We had no idea how he had injured his eye, but whatever had happened, his injury was severe. The nightmare continued for five weeks. Eye drops every two hours to a dog who didn't even like you to trim his toenails. We worked through that, and he was the best little patient but it was gut-wrenching. After the fifth week I'd thought the worst was over, only to have the vet say she didn't like what she was seeing and recommended that we take him to a veterinary ophthalmologist. The specialist confirmed what I had begun to suspect: Scout needed to have his eye removed. My sadness was immense. It flipped a switch for me.

We'd been watching my grandmother's health and mind decline to such a state that she no longer recognized us. Cleo Genevieve was a cornerstone in my life. She was part of my fabric; she had helped build my foundation. No matter how old I was, she had me on GPS. I used to (semi-jokingly) say that I was the only forty-year old woman whose grandmother knew where she was every moment. But I was glad she knew and glad she cared enough to want to know. When I was little I nick-named her Duke's Nannie after their dog, and she let me. I don't know too many women who would let you name them after a dog. I was her shadow. Although she was still technically "with" us, in actuality she was gone from us in all but breath. That's a hard grief to process. She'd been floating like a whisper in-between for months. The fragility and tenacity of life. I have no idea how her body continued to exist. Scout's accident tipped me over. It felt like two of my touchpoints had been stripped away.

Grief can bend us like straws, folding us as we try to cauterize the pain that threatens to shred the fiber of our being. Grief can force us into fetal positions as we try to turn inward, seeking solace from a world where loss lurks, waiting. I know from losing my father at a very young age that grief can lay dormant. It can shock you, how something can escape so many years later as if with the flip of a switch and grief just comes pouring out of you when you least expect it. They say grief has natural stages, the first being guilt, whether you have anything to feel guilty about or not. But to say grief has its stages is to imply that eventually it ends and is gone. It is not. Grief is like a well. You may think that your grief has run dry, but you'd be surprised to find untapped aquifers hidden hundreds of feet under the surface. Grief wells up at the most unexpected times and rends your flimsy concept of control with its intensity. I learned about grief early, and I have a feeling that that early loss burned itself on my brain like a brand. In spite of and maybe because of this, I describe myself as a wildly optimistic realist, but I think there's still some small singed corner of my brain that's certain it's just a matter of time until loss strikes again. That childhood well had tapped a gusher and I struggled to find my footing.

It was a complete blessing that we found veterinary ophthalmologist Dr. Rebecca Burwell and her wonderful staff. Rather than make me feel like I'd gone over the deep end twice – first to fall in love with a five pound dog and secondly to be so distraught over the loss of his tiny sparkly brown eye – they were competent and compassionate. The boys and I lobbied for a tiny false eye and Scout and I survived. He still wasn't an eye drop fan, but we made it through. Little did I know then that a few short months later it would be him taking care of me. There's something about a dog that soothes my soul. They live so completely in the moment. It's pretty hard to bum a dog out. They wake up every day excited about what's in store. They don't withhold affection, they bond strongly to those who love them, and they are amazingly loyal.

Disclaimer: A caveat about Kai. Kai is so lovable just about everyone we know has tried to take him home with them. Some friends have gone so far as to load him up into their cars. However, I saw a side of him during my recuperation that was a tiny bit disturbing. We'd adopted him the year prior and I'd been pretty certain he loved me the most, but I discovered during my recovery that he actually loves whoever walks him and throws a ball for him.

We love him immensely for the same reason; he may switch loyalties to follow the ball, but his whole existence is for love and fun. He loves to be outside, he loves to play; who can really blame him if he loves whoever loves those things too? I wasn't much use to him in my brace but we did develop a game where he would drop the tennis ball by my scruffy slippers and I would hold on to the pillar on the patio and kick the ball with my slipper. He had an amazing ability to put the ball exactly where I needed it and even though I could only kick the ball a few feet, he was as happy with that game as when I could throw the ball all the way down the hill.

Scout's recovery in his tiny newly one-eyed body was a poignant lesson. He weathered his own tragedy and came out the other side of it without any indication that it had broken him. He does have one little false eye, but you wouldn't know it. Those who know him well can see the slight hesitation when he's negotiating new territory, but no one else can tell. Everyone is surprised when we show off his eye. He had seemed so drawn into himself post-surgery that my heart was sick thinking he might never again be his old self. He has a habit where he runs into the house and leaps across the door mat into the entryway like a miniature dog superhero. It's just part of who he is, and I set that in my mind as a benchmark to whether, and when, he would return to us unscathed.

He did. Not only does he leap across the door mat again but he runs and plays and jumps just like he did before his accident. The arbitrary benchmarks I'd set of whether he was "okay" were based upon my intimate knowledge of his personality. He's fine. I'd bet the farm on it. So my question to me is, am I fine with it? Doctoring him through it, watching him lose one of his bright shiny button eyes tore the stuffing out of me. So am I okay with it? That seems to be the real question. I think it brings me full circle to all the things I love so much about dogs. I love their utter commitment to life. Every moment of it, the ugly and the beautiful. When they're happy, they're all the way happy. When they've been reprimanded, they take it and move on. Every day's a new day. Every day's a good day. They play hard, love all the way, and move on with whatever life hands them and don't let it get them down.

The three-legged dog and the one-eyed dog always bring me a smile and a slight tear. If they can still smile minus a couple of parts, who am I to begrudge my new titanium status? I can walk, I can smile, and I can love.

Scout's rebound gave me hope that I could make my own.

Chapter Twenty-Two
The Little Things

Notice the small things. The rewards are inversely proportional.
Liz Vassey

The early rains had passed and washed everything clean, lessening the threat of summer fires. A harvest moon had risen behind Mount Konocti, shining and huge. I saw it as I was hiking up the hill after doing chores and ran/walked into the house to get the male people to come outside to see it. All three broke away reluctantly from what they were doing; checking Facebook, playing the guitar, and watching ESPN. That wonderful family moment lasted about thirty seconds. Forget them. They might not care, but I stayed outside to absorb the gorgeous night. What a beautiful night. Beyond beautiful. A ten out of ten.

It's the little things, the small moments, I'm focusing on to fill me up when this recovery leaves me spent. Like the beauty of this morning, a perfect illustration of why I love the fall almost more than all the other seasons. The seasons all have their own allure, but fall combines them all. It's still warm, still a little cool. We may have rain and we may not. The horses are fuzzy with their impending winter coats but not miserable as they are in winter. It's hearty food weather, but you can still BBQ without freezing. Fall is good. The horses were waiting eagerly by the fence line, wondering why I'd passed them by as I finished my morning walk around the super highway. I'd snuck around the back way feeling guilty. Usually this is breakfast time but this morning I had to pass them by for the hay hose had run completely dry. Hay people can be kind of notorious for scheduling and the barn stood empty. All I could tell them was "Sorry guys, hay's coming" and hang my head and walk on by. When the hay arrived several hours later, their joyful chorus was hilarious. You'd think they were starving which wasn't funny considering that two of them are rescues and had experienced real starvation. It's probably a pretty disconcerting feeling to wonder if this is the day your hell returns. It was a good morning in the barn, the mud had dried and the air was crisp and all was well. I gave the old guys their morning ration for seniors and hay to everyone else. There are few sights I love more than the sight of horses lined up peacefully in their places, tossing beautiful hay around to find the best bits. They're completely at ease and all is well for another day. The dogs came down to the barn with me and got busy doing dog things. Unfortunately one of the most popular dog things is to look for tidbits of horse poop (Scout) and trying to eat out of the old guys' (Cassidy) buckets. Kai, the only civilized one, moseyed around the barn and did retriever things.

I'm trying to be quiet in my mind and peaceful in my thoughts while walking, rather than letting my thoughts clatter away like an old school typewriter, congealing all the frustrations of the day rather than appreciating the moment. Walking around the super highway again this evening, something made me think of clowns (too much caffeine?) and I could feel my mind slipping away from the perfection of the day and toward compiling a mental list of things I find creepy. Like clowns apparently. I remind myself of the vow I made in the hospital; that I would walk the superhighway again. I am in the very moment I longed for, but I'm wasting it on white noise. I let the quiet permeate my soul and calm the chatter in my head. One of the beautiful things in the aftermath was an almost excruciating sense of clarity jolting through my body like an IV infusion. Sometimes I can feel the intensity ebbing away from me as my regular life gets closer and my accident gets farther away. That's the essence of human nature it seems: to overlook the things right before us and to set our sight on the distance, our thoughts so far out in front of us that sometimes we miss what's right in front of us.

I can feel myself slipping just so slightly away from that marrow; that every moment needs to be experienced as if it's the only one, because, well, because it is.

I don't want to lose that lens of clarity in all things, the beautiful and the sad. Regardless of the anxiety and pain, the sense of being smack in the marrow of life was intense. I don't want to forget that. I don't want to give that up. I want to live my days as mindfully as I did in the aftermath when all I craved and clung to was the belief that someday I would be back in my "regular life", doing regular things and appreciating them all. Even ironing. Ironing is like chore yoga; it gets the wrinkles out of your clothes and your mind.

In spite of our universal knowledge that we bleed when cut, we can be so heedless of our finite days. It's false, that sense of security that a vast array of days lies out in front of us. Sometimes it's not until we're slammed into the wall to realize that we'd give anything to have back the day before the diagnosis became our new reality. It's an almost immediate sensation of the rarity and preciousness of the days that came before D day that we scramble madly to get back. I got a second chance and I don't want to ever forget that. I bank this moment in my soul.

Walking is my favorite part of the day. Each day I find I can walk a little faster and my body feels a little stronger. I walk as much as I can. No matter what time I head out it seems the deer are out to forage and look at me as if to say "You again?" They're congregated in a swale beneath the little hummock of a hill we call Gary's Knob (don't ask). A group of eighteen does and fawns look at each other trying to decide if they should run from me or not. Our favorite buck, a forked horn, is with them. He's a beauty, stout and broad. I don't know anything about deer language but I try to send out peaceful thoughts as they all notice me. I avert my eyes and try to walk by softly to let them know they can keep doing whatever deer things they're doing. They waver and don't scatter immediately, but the buck decides they should and they all bound up the hill. My command of deer language is obviously pretty poor.

There are huge new and unfamiliar footprints on the superhighway. My first thought was mountain lion. We do some research to check out its prints and it though it seems unlikely they're big cat tracks, they're still hecka big and a bit unnerving. The next morning they are almost washed away by the recent rains, but their shadow remains. I'd been reprimanded (deservedly) for not carrying a cell phone or wearing a helmet the day of my accident, and I'm trying to make up for it. I'm carrying a whistle, cell phone, and pepper spray. Riot gear. My mom would be happy. As I walk by the huge prints it dawns on me that a mountain lion could very well be in the area. Riders around here have reported sightings in the past. Fortunately, a bobcat is the largest cat I've seen on our property which was pretty cool. It occurred to me that if a mountain lion thought I looked tasty, I might come to an untimely end or a mild mauling while doing nothing more adventurous than walking. The realization comes to me, unlikely but not impossible, that I could be messed up doing nothing more adventurous than walking. People have choked to death on movie popcorn. The realization that sometimes things just happen no matter what you're doing begins to put some of my residual fear into perspective.

Some of the best guides along this journey have been the animals around me. The dogs' heartfelt approach to each day has helped anchor me to the salient essence of life and to find the joy before me. The horses have kept me tied to passion over fear; that in spite of being hurt doing the thing I love best; they are helping me find my way back to that passion. Bit by bit. Today it's some unknown animal, walking the superhighway just as we are but I appreciate the lesson. Stuff happens. Some we seek out and some just finds us.

And, whatever or whoever you are, thanks for not eating me.

Chapter Twenty-Three

Wise Guys and Knuckle Heads

How do you catch a loose horse? - Make a noise like a carrot.
Unknown

Six horses legitimately qualify as a herd. I really never intended to end up with half a dozen, but somehow one horse rapidly turned into two and then two into four, and somehow number five came with a "buy one get one makes six" kind of a deal I couldn't pass up. The best intentions just fall by the wayside sometimes. The hay hose is constantly on around here. I hesitate to do the actual math involved in the upkeep of six horses. The six can be neatly divided into two groups of three: wise guys and knuckleheads. The wise guys aren't fazed by much and the knuckle heads tend to get worked up easily. But sometimes even the wise guys take their cue from the knuckleheads and get led astray.

The best illustration of the wise guy/knucklehead break-down is the day I came home from taking my sons into town for school. As I drove down our gravel drive way I thought to myself "Hmm, wonder where those horses are?" The boys and I operated on a no-minute-to-spare approach to getting to school on time (keys misplaced, homework forgotten until we'd hit the paved road, hectic mornings with lives of their own) so there was no time to investigate. Returning home I realized that if the horses weren't all lined up in place waiting to be fed, then there's probably a pretty good reason. They were absolutely nowhere to be found. This made me a little bit crabby. I grabbed one halter, a bucket, and six horse cookies and hit the superhighway in search. Why only one halter? That's a really good question for which I have no really good answer. Not enough coffee? In my mind I was thinking it unlikely that I could catch and lead all six horses at one time. Up to that point four ponies had been my limit. My plan was to get one hooked up and lure the rest with the irresistible sound of cookies jiggling around in the bucket. Every horse loves a bucket. I dare you to find an exception. I set off, one halter, six cookies to find six horses.

I wasn't moving too quickly those days so I figured this manhunt might take a while. After walking clear around the animal superhighway and getting crabbier by the minute, I spied a spot of bright red peeking out from the creek bed. Found them. The grass is always greener across the creek it seems. After hearing the clang of the cookies in the bucket one of the perpetrators, Simba (a wise guy), gratefully gave himself up in exchange for a cookie. The other perps took more persuading but it's hard to hide when you're wearing a bright red blanket. The rest of them were really starting to piss me off. I decided I could be happy enough with just Simba. Simba was happily munching cookies so he and I headed back down the trail home. Simba might be able to count because he knew there were more cookies in the bucket and he was perfectly happy to be the sole recipient of them. Back we headed; Simba happy to have been saved from a life in the wilds and me clanking the remaining cookies in the bucket to give the knuckleheads some motivation to return if they so desired.

By this point I had decided that if the five of them wanted to return to their wild roots, it was fine with me. Pat already thought six horses were a bit much, so maybe this was the answer? I was about out of cookies as Simba was happily working his way through them when the stragglers staged a stampede. I heard them come tearing up behind us and turned around to see a raggedy bunch of horses who'd decided their wild days were over. I ignored the lot of them while Simba and I kept walking back to the pasture and the other five followed us somewhat shame-faced.

Funny how a horse can bust out of an electric fence, but there's no way they ever seem to put themselves back in.

Chapter Twenty-Four

Birthday Suit

Life is good today.
Zac Brown Band

I woke early to the sound of two ravens having some kind of a party outside my window. They'd been especially noisy lately and I didn't know what gives. Maybe it's because I had saved one of their brethren who'd been drinking from the horses' water trough and had accidently fallen in. I'd found him one morning, only his beak sticking out above the water line, as I'd gone down to check on the water. Ravens are big, much bigger up close than you'd think. I had no prior experience in raven saving. He looked pretty desperate, so I grabbed two long sticks and tried to make some makeshift chopsticks to lift him out. He hissed at me when I got close and I told him, "look, you don't have many options, buddy," and he immediately quieted down. I managed to balance his water-logged chest against the first chopstick, and he put his feet up on the lower stick as I lifted him out and set him down next to the trough. He was surprisingly heavy and completely saturated with water. He stood dazed for a moment, and then shook his feathers and waddled away to rest under an oak tree. Maybe he was one of the noisy duo, and maybe this early song-fest was his way of saying thank you. Maybe they knew it was my birthday and were singing happy birthday to me, raven style.

Sometimes you have to do a reality check as you wake to clear away whatever your brain had been dreaming about and to bring your brain back from wherever it had gone during the night. A wave of sadness washed over me as the reality check reminded me how un-wonderful my body felt and flooded into my now awake brain. Birthdays had been a lot more fun twenty years ago. Birth-day had been more like a week of celebrating. Now, my body felt weak and I wanted it to feel strong. I shook off the poor me that was trying to settle in and got up, got the dogs, and headed down to the barn to feed. All six horses were looking at me like "Let's get this party started" which chased some of the sad out of me.

Usually the two old guys are the only ones who get a bucket filled with anything special, but lately everybody seems to be in some state of special needs. The old guys get their Elk Grove stable mix senior plus this new thing I was trying called Renew Gold. They dance around like two crack heads, running back and forth along the fence line. It seems like everything they're getting is working, because they are fresh as five year olds. Wish gets a special mix for her mild case of laminitis. Luke is getting Silver Lining Herbs Infection 25X to settle down his swollen sheath which happens every summer when the first hot days hit. I wouldn't doubt his condition is providing provocative conversation for anyone riding the trail along our prop-erty line because it's pretty hard to miss. Sundance gets a bucket too, because who wants to be the only guy not getting any? The dogs sit patiently in the barn watching me watch me mix the magic potions, staying out of the early morning heat. It's going to be hot today; they can already feel it coming.

Everybody loves a bucket. I balance all the buckets, trying to remember which order they are in, and all the horses line up at the fence, in a state of such anticipation that I feel like the most popular person in the world. The adoration is making me feel much happier. Hoot stretches in a downward dog pose. I'm impressed he's so good at yoga; I had no idea. He'd just started doing this and he's pretty darn flexible. Luke's bucket comes with a caveat; as he's eating I whip out the hose and start spraying cold water on his sheath. He's a really good sport as it would seem that having your private parts sprayed with cold water is a pretty harsh way to start the day. He thinks the bucket's a good trade-off and he puts up with me hosing him off without making a big deal about it.

Wish and Sundance eat peacefully side by side, minding their own business and enjoying their buckets. I run my hand over Wish's withers and sneak a sniff. She's sun-warmed as I put my nose down into the delicious smell of her and feel the still gentle sun on my face. My internal switch re-sets and my spirit fills with the feel of being in a perfect moment. Back at the house I feed the dogs and play Frisbee with Kai for a bit. As I put the Frisbee away, I find two little frogs sitting under the other Frisbee. I smile again. This day is turning out a lot better than I thought. Small things really, but to my raggedy heart they feel big. We struggle over so many things, searching for ways to fill the holes life gouges in our hearts and souls. My realization over this journey has been that the small things of an ordinary day help fill in those holes. My soul smiles and embraces the reality of right here, right now, in all its imperfection and beauty and my (birth) day begins.

I'm excited and kind of anxious because I have a date this morning. My quest to get back in the saddle has led me on an exploration of body protectors which is all new to me as I've never ridden with anything like that, except sporadic use of a helmet (sorry, Mom). As my healing progressed, I'd begun deconstructing the riding equation and sought to make each variable as safe as possible. I'll always miss the feeling of riding in a baseball cap and t-shirt, but that's not an option I'm comfortable with now. I realize that anything to do with horses is inherently dangerous, and I owe it to those I love to do it as responsibly and safely as possible. The call of the horse is too strong for me to ignore; it's a part of my being. Riding is still riding, and horses are still horses, and I am doing due diligence by trying to make all the variables as safe as I possibly can.

My date's with Wendy McCaughan of KanTeq in Ireland. Wendy has spent years researching body protectors and different materials and how they react during the impact of a fall. Her designs are modeled after motocross wear technology and utilize unique foam with the ability to absorb and disseminate the energy of a fall, rather than recoiling upon impact. Her body protectors are designed specifically for women. We've been emailing back and forth and this morning we had a date to Skype and go over the specifics for my own Kan protector.

Our date was for 8:00 a.m. my time, 3:00 p.m. Ireland. I made tea (the Irish love their tea so it seemed fitting) and got on Skype. Miraculously she answered right off just like she was next door and we began. The beauty of her accent made me smile, and my smile was still on my face when we hung up, forty-eight minutes later. We talked about technology, we talked about injuries, we talked about science and engineering and energy transformation, and dogs. I told her that it was my birthday and that I honestly couldn't think of anything that would make me happier today than knowing that I have taken an enormous, pivotal step to getting back in the saddle. What seemed like a grim reminder of how far I had slipped in all things that had made me feel like me was being replaced with a sense of going forward. Feelings I'd despaired of feeling again like hope and a feeling of such gratitude that there's someone out there doing what Wendy does to make the best possible piece of protection (or "kit" as she so charmingly called it) so that people like me can go forward. Reading the testimonials on Wendy's site I found other people, just like me, who couldn't imagine not riding. Wendy's world helped me realize that I'm not alone in my fears and in my desire to ride again, "kitted" up this time.

We're born naked into the world clad only in what we've come to call our birthday suits. Mine was a lot less travelled back then and had a lot fewer scars. I'd been blessed with good health and a strong body for so many years and it had served me well. I'd felt strong and able and had done so many things without a thought of it. My body had met whatever challenges I threw at it from skiing down the (smallest chute) Palisades at Squaw Valley to surfing (poorly) in Costa Rica, and jumping off the cliffs at Lake Berryessa (a result of my lack of good sense in college). Now my body and I have a different relationship. I remind myself how blessed I am to be walking, let alone to even be able to consider riding again.

I am thankful for the blessing of a second chance.

I email Wendy to thank her again for her time and encouragement, and it dawns on me. My new body protector is my new birthday suit. I chose black over blue so that I could look like a real ninja this time around. I'll wear it knowing that while my real birthday suit isn't quite as pristine as the one I came with, that I am really doing this.

I am going to ride again. *I am going to ride again.* Scars and all.

Chapter Twenty-Five

Hands

I have held many things in my hands, and I have lost them all;
but whatever I have placed in God's hands, that I still possess.
Martin Luther

Not long after I was able to travel again, we found ourselves back in the hospital. This time we were the visitors and we were there to visit a friend who'd been shot in the chest at close range in a senseless act of violence. Our community was stunned that this peaceful man had been the victim of such a horrible act of violence. Violence only happens to strangers, right? He had been flown in a REACH helicopter to the same hospital that I'd been taken to for trauma stabilization.

Walking down the same hallways I'd been rolled through was

eerie. This time, I was the one who was upright and we were there to see our friend with a hole in his chest from a .40 caliber handgun. I'd spent most of my stay there flat on my back, so what was very familiar turf to Pat wasn't to me because of our different perspectives. His time in the hospital had been primarily vertical while mine had been mostly horizontal.

What we thought would be a brief visit had turned into several hours, and we realized it was his way of processing the horror. He needed to talk. His words poured out as he sought to explain to us and to himself the events that had lead up to the shooting. I don't believe our bodies or our minds are programmed to process trauma of such violence. It is almost as if our bodies reject the information and then keep pulling it back, regurgitated, to somehow get it processed in a way that we can absorb. My back was aching and my mind was overloaded, as I tried to make sense of senselessness. Déjà vu flooded over me.

I looked down at my hands as I listened and had one of those weird moments of wondering "Who am I and how did I get here?" The hands I saw didn't look like my own hands but like those of my mother. I don't spend much time contemplating my hands. But I had trouble reconciling that these were really my own. They looked like the work-worn hands of my mom, a farmer's wife and a woman who is never still. Hands tell our story. My father's strong work-tough hands tell the story of a farmer and a builder. My husband's hands make mine look childlike in comparison, but they tell his story of making things happen, the hands of a doer. I blinked to clear my eyes and try to refocus my brain, but my mom's hands were still there. Mine had the same shape, the same tan, the same feel to them that I get when I look at her hands.

It was hard to reconcile that my hands looked just like my mom's. I'd long ago read a semi-fictional book about King Henry VIII and the author's description of how he'd disliked his hands as they began to age; the diamond crisscross of skin that had seen time. I love 15th and 16th century English history. It doesn't hurt that most historical movies have really awesome horses too. Unlike Henry VIII, I spend very little time focused on how my hands look. My fingernails are afterthoughts. I also use them as tools even though I know I shouldn't. It's a rare day I'm not mixing some kind of supplements to keep weight on the two oldest horses as they age. Consequently, I often have brown mush stuck under my nails. I don't wear rings other than my wedding ring because I use my hands and they look like it. I've only had real girl nails twice. At fifteen, my family took a month-long trip to China. Maybe it was the lack of daily work or a diet high in protein, but I had some serious nails when we came home. Years ago, I received a birthday gift certificate for gel nails. Obviously the giver had recognized that I needed help. I still remember walking out to my car trying to work the clicker with nails. My fingers looked (and felt) so foreign. I didn't navigate these nails well. They looked gorgeous: bright red and super sexy. I couldn't stop looking at them. They were mesmerizing. They were beautiful but it wasn't an effort that I could muster up, so in a few short weeks my red nails were gone.

In the hospital again, this time on the other side of the situation, my hands spoke to me. I've never really thought that I looked like my mom, but I'm not averse to seeing her in my hands. My mom is a beautiful and hard-working woman. She comes from a long line of hard-working people. They are helpers: people who bring dinner to the sick and who visit the lonely; people who drove to far away states each year to help aging family; people you could count on to help you garden, farm, move, and comfort. Those are the kind of people I come from. Looking down now and seeing that my hands reflect that heritage, makes me happy, not sad. I'll never be a hand model but that's not my story either. My hands tell my story as well as that of my people; our hands are nurturers hands. People who've nurtured the soil, and animals, and family. I could feel that love in the hands of my mother, and of her mother, and her father.

They may not be pretty, but I found that didn't matter. I use my hands to navigate through my day. Feel is what matters to me. Feel is important in working with animals. That light responsiveness of the leash when you're walking a happy dog that's right with you in stride and spirit. Making a loop in a rope that feels balanced just right. The feel I've struggled to find in my reins as I ride. I grew up trying to mimic the loose rein that the cool cowboys rode with in westerns. When I began to learn more, I learned how my reins can be used as a conversation with my horse. Not by pulling on them or throwing them away, but by creating a connection that allows the pace and tone of our conversation to change effortlessly without disconnecting, calling back, or starting over. The times where I've finally gotten that give and take right have been powerful and addictive. The times you connect to a horse with real feel makes you want more, makes you want that connection all the time. It is the why, to why do we ride.

Feel is what matters. How we express love through our touch. How we communicate with our humans and our horses through touch. The incredible feeling of holding the reins just right and the comforting feel of holding a hand. Horse and human. Hands convey our silent communication with each other. Our hands allow us out to join another, holding each other to this spinning earth. Grounding us and anchoring us to another as if to say I won't let go; we will be okay. The healing power that exists in a gentle touch; a diffusion of kindness. I've been so blessed to feel so much through my hands, even if they look worse for wear. They've felt joys and sorrows. My hands have experienced the indescribable feeling of holding a stunned hummingbird, to the sorrow of holding a friend's hand when no words remain to say how sorry you are that her marriage has imploded and that her husband is a total ass leaving her pregnant to figure out where to go from there. My hands have held the beautiful little hands of my boys and felt a love so powerful that even now recollecting the feel of their tiny hands in mine makes me yearn to rewind the clock, if only I could feel their tiny hands in mine one more time.

How incredible that the same body part, with different intent, can produce such different results. The hand that acted against our friend created violence and bloodshed, all started by a finger that should have never been on that trigger. My own hand holding onto my grandmother's hand; her skin thin as paper as she lay slowly dying. Words didn't work anymore. All I had left to give her was the love of a lifetime I was trying to transmit from my hand to hers; to try to reach her in that faraway place her mind had taken her when it left us behind. I still remember her hand holding mine as a child. I remember her hand toasting me with her favorite Manhattans as we both grew older. She may not have known my hand as she slowly left us, but I knew hers. I held on as if it were possible to hold on tightly enough to keep from being left without her. She is gone from me now, but my memories stay alive fueled by the memory of that touch. My saving memory is that she never knew about my accident. It would have broken her heart.

So many lessons in the hospital. The déjà vu of being back in the same hospital, this time as a visitor, brought me unexpected lessons in time, heritage, and love. My hands are simple and unadorned but they're mine. Now I could see my mother and my grandmother in them, and feel their love in me. The déjà vu cleared and my hands looked like mine again. They've covered a lot of territory - climbed rocks, tried to knit and failed, clapped at hundreds of soccer and baseball games, and itched to give a few "you're number one signs" but mostly resisted.   I have also felt the hands of God holding me from the moment that I found myself in the air when the rabbit began its run and set this whole journey in motion.

Chapter Twenty-Six

Blink

Children are the hands by which we take hold of heaven.
Henry Ward Beecher

Max, my eldest son, is somehow 6'2" and going off to college. He's headed east, accepted into the program of his dreams. He's ready. I couldn't be prouder of him but it feels like just yesterday he turned eighteen and moved invisibly from being my child to becoming an adult. I watched him drive off, taking his brother into town to school. Other people on the road that morning saw two brothers in a car. I saw a lifetime of love enclosed in a steel container. I thought of all that can go wrong in this world, all that reminds us of our fragility in a world that gives and takes away. Sometimes the residue of fear lingering in the aftermath of my wreck threatens to take hold of me, and I realize that the lasting vestiges of my accident linger like sneaking fog fingers inside me. My physical being is mending, but the emotional mending is a bit trickier. There goes my heart in that car and I know I can only do so much to protect them. Let go. That's my job now. It sounds so reasonable but in truth, well, in truth it hurts. What is that work of a lifetime, raising a child? As with horsemanship, I have had to figure my way through motherhood too. I was completely clueless about babies and kids. Max was born almost six weeks early, arriving right before Thanksgiving rather than being the Christmas baby we'd expected. Fortunately Pat knew what to do so he grabbed ahold of that tiny baby in his big solid hands and wrapped him up like a burrito, a modern day spin on swaddling, and got him kick started so that I could see that it could be done without breaking him. Being my sons' mom has been my greatest joy. I was a total rookie when I was blessed with them. I've made mistakes. I've learned great lessons along the journey of motherhood. Nothing I have ever done has meant more to me than loving and raising them. Motherhood is a servant's journey, requiring an adventurer's heart and a comedian's attitude.

I've made Rice Krispy Treats only once, a fact that I am both proud of, and embarrassed by. Kids love Rice Krispy Treats but I just couldn't. Hopefully I made up for it in other ways. Early on I learned the humbling power of admitting that you have made a mistake and owe your child an apology. If I can't apologize to them when I am wrong, how can I expect them to do so when they are? A heartfelt apology is one of the greatest gifts we can give and receive. I teetered on the brink of that realization when they were little boys – realizing that I'd blown it and needed to ask them for their forgiveness for my short-temper as I had yelled at them and saw their tender little faces crumple as they too realized that I was human, made of weak flesh and blood. I'll never forget the day I realized that I stood at a critical junction. I could pull the "I'm the adult card," or I could tell them that yelling at them was never okay. In my great mom dreams I always talked to them calmly and wisely, just like Yoda, but in reality sometimes I was plain tired and short-tempered as I tried to figure out where they ended and I began. It hurt to admit that I had let them down, but apologizing to them when I have is one of the things of motherhood that I know I have done exactly right.

Eighteen years had crawled and flown by. I watched my sons drive away. Now I'm hanging on to the tail of our time together and watching from the side-lines when I was once at the heart of it. That journey to independence is the natural progression of things and how it needs to be. Somehow, right now, knowing that just doesn't make it any easier. I look at the world before my sons and wonder how they will navigate through to find their own way. I can only guide them so much before they make their own lives. I pray that the wrong things take a back-seat to the good things and that they'll make right choices that will keep them upright and keep them from the remorse of bad choices and the pain of wrong turns. We took our own detours and made our own bad calls, and we wish that our words spurred from our own wounds would keep our kids from making their own mistakes, but life doesn't work that way. Words are just words until experience makes them wisdom. I realize that I can worry all day long or I can pray.

With my bittersweet realization today comes a wash of tears and a lifetime of a love I wouldn't trade for anything. I stand on the precipice of letting them go to find their own lives and to leave behind the one we lived together. It's been said that to have a child is to forever have your heart go walking around outside your body. My heart will never be my own and I wouldn't trade that for anything. Long ago when I felt I couldn't keep up with the energy of little boys another day I wish someone much wiser had told me that those busy days pass by way too quickly. Count them as joy.

Breathe. Treasure. Love.

There goes my heart in that car. I wish someone had told me then to keep my eyes open and to never blink.

Motherhood, as with horsemanship, is a never ending journey, stanchioned by the same bookends of blazing truth and searing love.

Chapter Twenty-Seven
Soul Sisters

I get by with a little help from my friends.
The Beatles

Nothing puts your own tragedy in quite so much perspective as far greater tragedy. Two months after (what was to me) my life-altering accident, Japan was rocked by a series of incomprehensibly powerful earthquakes. The undersea megathrust earthquake registered 9.1 on the Richter scale. The Richter scale is a logarithmic scale, meaning that an increase isn't an increase of just one; each whole number represents an increase of ten-fold. To put that into perspective, I've read that a Richter 10 quake would be so powerful it could literally rend a continent in half. San Francisco's 1906 earthquake had a magnitude of 7.8 and destroyed over 80% of the city. Japan's earthquake was so powerful it actually moved Honshu the main island of Japan and actually shifted the axis of the earth. Moments later a tsunami of epic proportion wrecked further destruction as it ripped the shores. The tsunami then triggered nuclear accidents at three nuclear plants causing 100,000s of people to be evacuated. The world reeled at the magnitude of the destruction. Tragedy reminds us of our frailty, of the Latin phrase *memento mori* "remember death", and of our mortal transience. It's not just global tragedy that rocks our worlds. It seems that everyday something reminds us of the fragility of our lives. Sometimes it's just a matter of how close to home it hits. I'd just learned about a young mother who willingly underwent premature delivery of her fourth child so that she could fight Stage 4 breast cancer without harming her yet unborn baby.

But within tragedy is the opportunity to learn how and who you want to be. It illuminates the power of the people in your life. Within my own tragedy I was blessed beyond measure by the actions of my family and friends. It gives me the desire to repay those blessings when tragedy strikes those around me. When I'd finally been admitted to ICU, Pat began the unenviable task of making calls. Within moments of those calls, friends from far and near descended upon my hospital room. Writing those words brings tears of appreciation and acknowledgement of how powerful that circle of friends has been in my life: before the crash and most poignantly, after.

My childhood friend Leslie drove immediately from her home in Sacramento. Deb made the tricky trek over Highway 17 through rush hour traffic. My sister-in-law Katie came from her home right around the corner and sat with me every morning at 5 a.m. until my parents arrived to take their turn. My sister-in-law Amy got on the first plane out of Texas and sat by my bedside late every night until I could fall asleep. For nine days she did this. As payback she says I babbled to her about the history of HeLa cell lines, an odd conversation topic which I blame totally on the drugs. Val left a family celebration to bring me tulips and candy and movies. Laura brought her wonderful mom. Terri brought books and my first bottle of wine for after the pain meds were done. Stephanie called our horse friends, and their calls came pouring in from all over. Somehow Shannon managed to make me laugh every day. My college friend and fellow horse lover Beth drove up for the day, just to give me a hug. Jeri came up from southern California and stayed for four days. She brought her optimism and mad-crazy organizational skills. We share a love for super obscure mid-18th century literature and she actually read to me and we laughed at what major geeks we are.

Jeri is an old soul and I value her observations. She said "Everything can happen. I look at each day as a cool new adventure." She should know. She's endured more than her fair share of tragedies. She's done it with incredible strength and resilience and she's maintained an openness and optimism I treasure. Debbie would come over to baby-sit me, bringing my favorite Starbuck's mocha with her. Her quiet support and calm presence lent me strength when I was lacking and lifted me up when I was down. She took on some wifely duties and put a big smile on Pat's face by ironing his shirts. I never iron so that was a big deal around here. I could see the benefit in sister wives. If we could find a woman who would be happy to iron for him, I'd be totally up for that.

Paula had rushed to the ER to pray for me. When I was home she'd show up with cleaning supplies and get busy. She also brought Starbuck's so by this time not only did I feel blessed beyond measure but seriously caffeinated too. It was obvious I have a real talent for picking great friends. She was the one who decided I needed to get out of the house when two months had passed, and she took me out, brace and all. You know you've been out of commission when a trip to the Grocery Outlet thrills you more than anything has in a long time. The list goes on. My mom came to stay for several weeks to make sure I was eating prunes and to help out around the house. Pat's mom brought delicious food. Notes of kindness poured in from our ag community and church, delicious dinners were delivered for months, and the ongoing wave of love astounded me. I will never be able to say enough to express my gratitude for the love which surrounded me and my family during this time.

Trauma's tricky. You may think that if you leave it alone, it will go away. It won't. One thing I'd learned during this season of recovery was how important it was to acknowledge our trauma, the physical and the emotional, so that we can look at it full on and work our way through it. If you ignore it, it will eventually jump out at you. Just like the rabbit. I'd found that out the hard way with my second run-in with a rabbit. I'd been thinking that my physical self was all that needed mending, but the reenactment of the rabbit showed me that I had emotional trauma needing mending too. Some of this mending only you can do your own, but so much comes from those who love you and stand by your side when you're scared and unsure of what's next or how this will all unwind. Sometimes you just can't fix what happened. Sometimes all you can do is just show up. Some wounds are so deep and raw they just have to be lived through. Sometimes there just aren't words that will help fix some of the wrecks we get into, but love always heals. Sometimes our wrecks leave us in tatters, but our friends can help stitch together the pieces with their love, just like an old time quilting bee.

My soul sisters showed up. I'd always wanted a big boisterous family but I'm an only. Nature didn't grant that wish but friendship did and my friend family filled that spot. Don't get me wrong; I mean no disrespect to my male friends and I love them dearly too. I have to mention Richard here as otherwise he will ask me why I did not. But there is a special place in my heart for my soul sisters and how nurture, rather than nature, forged our kinship. My soul sisters make up a big, rambunctious, colorful, and never-boring soul family. They figuratively circled the wagons and their friendship, laughter, and love helped lift me up when I was at my lowest. Their friendships shined like night lights on the path as I've crawled back from my own personal crash and burn helped me to find the life lessons nestled within.

Chapter Twenty-Eight

First Ride

You can ride me.
Simba

      Simba came into my life through the horse hotline. I'd come to know a group of women involved in horse rescue through Stephanie; Steph's a defense attorney by day and a horse advocate every other moment. I named it the horse hotline as it was an email connecting horse lovers from all over to help place horses in need. The list has expanded beyond horses and often includes goats, dogs, and an occasional potbellied pig or chicken.

One day an email for an older palomino gelding landed in my inbox. Times were tough, and in tough times horses tend to be among the first things to go when people are having trouble making ends meet. Simba lived down the road from the women who rescued him. They drove by daily and their concern mounted as they saw his condition deteriorating. He'd been living on a pile of rocks with a tethered goat as his only companion. Food was pretty much non-existent for the two of them, so Roni and Angie stepped in. His owner was struggling to keep him and gratefully accepted their help. They nursed Simba (and his goat) back to health and set about finding a new home for him. They were familiar with Simba, an older quarter horse who'd had a rough go on the local gymkhana circuit and had been passed through too many different owners. They were looking to place him in a forever home so he could get the new start he deserved.

Simba had stuck in my heart. Just two months prior, on a cold December morning just days before Christmas, I'd gone down to feed, and my gelding Skeeter hadn't come to meet me. He was always the first to greet me. You learn quickly, if the animals aren't in their usual places waiting for food. My heart sunk. I fed the other horses and crawled through the fence to search for him. Skeeter was in the far pasture, cold and gone. My knees buckled and I dropped down to touch him, desperate to find some indication of life; something to tell me the horrible picture in front of me was wrong and that he wasn't gone. Our bodies know loss and tragedy sometimes long before our minds wrap themselves around truths we don't want to embrace. My heart was sick. Without Skeeter, my horse mojo was gone. Skeeter was my go-to guy and my partner. My soul was sick too, that I'd missed any signs of colic. I flogged myself with guilt over the thought that I'd left him to die alone on a cold winter night. Grief knocked the oomph out of my riding. I just couldn't. I lost that desire and spent two months feeding horses rather than riding horses. I was just done.

Weeks passed since I'd read that email, but one day I had business near where Simba was being fostered, so I asked if I could meet him. My outfit wasn't the best for horse visiting, but heels don't slow country girls down, not even remotely. I climbed through the fence, just as I had when I'd gone searching for Skeeter but this time and this fence; I found Simba and fell in love. Through a minor (and possibly honest) misrepresentation of Simba's size, I told Pat this horse should live with us and could perhaps someday, be Pat's horse. Roni and Angie vetted me through shared acquaintances and allowed me to take Simba. Pat took one look at Simba the day they delivered him, and realized that I'd been wearing my horse goggles that day. Pat is a big guy and Simba, well not so much. Kind of like that engraving on passenger side mirrors, objects in mirror are closer than they appear. That same wonky perception was at work the day I fell in love with Simba.

Sometimes love and redemption come from unexpected places.

Simba was in his high teens and had recurrent laryngeal neuropathy (RLN) commonly called "roaring." RLN is an obstructive upper airway disorder of horses, resulting when the cricoarytenoid dorsalis (CAD) muscle and the nerve which supplies it don't function properly and can manifest as laryngeal paralysis. The CAD muscle is the one that opens the larynx during exercise. The larynx isn't able to fully function, hence the roaring sound made by animals suffering from this condition. As I began to research what this meant to Simba, I learned that although this condition is critical in racing and performance horses, it shouldn't be an issue with light recreational riding. Simba joined my herd and became the old gentleman of the group. We began to get to know each other. He was hyper-aware and sensitive to anything I asked of him, or even what he anticipated I might ask of him, as if he were afraid not to do exactly what was expected. He was fearful of ropes and anything around his legs. Day by day we learned more about each other. Day by day he became to believe that this was his real home and he would have the food he needed. He knew he was safe. It takes horses longer than we give them credit for to believe that they are truly home.

Simba is one of the most expressive horses I've ever known. He's like an old mustachioed grandpa. After he was fully-recovered we took our first ride together, a simple little walk on part of the superhighway. My neighbor Huia came over to ride with us. I saddled up and gently got on, and off we went. Simba started to grumble almost immediately. I was convinced that those two steps we'd taken must have activated his RLN, which was obviously more serious than I'd thought. We stopped riding and the grumbling stopped. We moved; grumbling. It wasn't long before I learned that he was actually grumbling. If he didn't like something, riding or not, he would grumble. Once I tuned in to Simba's sensitivity and his vocal way of communicating with me, I realized he had things he needed me to hear. I don't think he'd spent much of his life being heard. He challenged me to communicate with him, on a level I'd never tried before. It was as if I could hear his thoughts. I tried to clear my own noisy human head and communicate with him, without words. We tend to be noisy in our communication with horses, which is quite opposite of how horses communicate with each other. This was the first time a horse used noises to communicate with a noisy human like me.

It was weird. Weird, but incredible.

As he began to realize that his new life wasn't like his old life, and that I actually cared about how he felt about things, his grumbling stopped almost immediately. If he would grumble, I'd tell him (silently) "Let's just try a little....." and his grumbling would stop. Day by day he relaxed. Simba became the most endearing horse. It was Simba who would let me cry into his shedding hair and Simba who welcomed me each day with a nicker just for me. No more grumbles, just a happy nicker.

I knew it couldn't be Wish for my first ride. No ill-will towards her, just way too much emotion there. I'd been taking steps towards the day when I could and would ride again, but "who" was the big question mark. My neurosurgeon had given my recovery a year before I'd be officially off his books and on my own. I'd done PT and acupuncture for months, and I felt ready. I had my Kan body protector, the helmet my folks bought me; I just didn't have any clue who could help me make this comeback ride. I'd been talking Pat's ear off and conferring with my horse friends, but nothing. The horses had been pretty much retired for a whole year. One afternoon I was spending time with Simba, just brushing him and hanging out when I heard, clear as verbalized words, "Ride me." It felt pretty much like a horse had just spoken to me. Ride me. Simba, old rescue horse, offered to be my first ride.

All I'd been thinking about was riding again, but now that it was here, I was stumped as to how to do this. To actually put my leg over a horse again after the trauma of the past year plus would require an extra-special horse to absorb the emotions and a calm and care I could count on.

"Ride me." Clear as a bell. Riding wasn't like it used to be; there was no just throwing a saddle on by myself and heading out. Riding had turned into the proverbial dog and pony show. Pat saddled for me and I had all kinds of external hardware to put on. The vest felt like my suit of armor, providing physical and mental reinforcement. My helmet felt weird compared to a ball cap. I had to use a mounting block rather than getting on from the ground. Simba waited patiently through all my fumbling and flopping around. Finally: I was ready. Standing on the mounting block felt like standing on the top of a high dive and wondering if you'd do a clean dive or belly flop. Waiting there I felt just born and ancient, but nothing like the old me. Ride me. Simba turned his head toward me and gently reminded me that we were in this together. I put my foot in the stirrup and after a moment's pause, threw my leg over.

I was in the saddle. After the endless days of prayer (more prayer), anxiety and fear, I was in the saddle. I sat still and soaked in the keen reality of it. During those dark nights when the elephant threatened to crush my chest as well as my spirit, I'd despaired that this day would ever come. It had: one year and a half after my unexpected dismount. Yep, I was bundled up like a baby or a hockey player, but I was in the saddle. Underneath me Simba let me know he was taking care of me. Pat and Cassidy waited expectantly, and off we went, a real live dog and pony show: Me, my sweet guide Simba, my husband and my dog. We all walked around and up and down our drive a bit and called it good. I was ecstatic. My legs buckled as I realized I'd been trembling and I sat on the mounting block as feelings washed over me and I tried to adequately express to Pat what had happened. "As soon as I threw my leg over the saddle, I could feel the broken pieces start to come back together." It wasn't just physical.

My spirit had gotten disconnected from my body too.

I couldn't wait to ride again. Like tomorrow. This time Simba told me "Okay." The next afternoon we repeated the dog and pony show, and as my leg was mid-air over the saddle I could feel my soul and body move just a little bit closer together. Joy flooded my heart. Pat, Cassidy, Simba, and I set off for the same kind of ride. We didn't cover much physical ground but I could tell I was covering acres of emotional ground.

I was ready to do this every day.

The third day Simba looked slightly less enthusiastic. After our ride, clear as a bell he said, "Okay. That's enough."

He was in his late twenty's by now; he'd been with me for almost ten years. We'd never been certain of his age but we knew he was older when he came to us. Simba was happy being retired. I can appreciate that. His old life hadn't been the easiest and he loved his new life. He saved me when I needed saving and he got me back in the saddle. Thanks to his gentle care, I wasn't incapacitated by the fear of getting back in the saddle. That barrier had been overcome. Just as I'd learned about his grumbling when we first met, I also learned that his non-grumbling communication was just as clear. I thanked him for the rides and took him at his word.

Ride me. Life is full of unexpected journeys. Who would have thought that when I adopted an old palomino horse, that same horse ten years later would be my guide out of the darkness and back into the saddle? I love him. I will miss Simba when he's ready to go. He has taught me so much about horsemanship and resilience. And life. I'll forever be grateful. I hope he lives to be fifty.

Chapter Twenty-Nine

Sunspot

To see the world in a grain of sand, and to see heaven in a wild flower,
hold infinity in the palm of your hands, and eternity in an hour.
William Blake

We can learn a lot from dogs if only we pay attention. A dog's whole existence is based on several seemingly simple principles. My favorite dog-taught lesson is in how they embrace the moment, no matter how simple. Take Scout for example. Scout's taking advantage of the sunny weather after days of early rain. He's found a sunspot in our bedroom and is soaking up the warmth, all four little legs stretched out full-length, eyes closed. He looks so perfectly content that I can't stop myself from kneeling down to look more closely. He stretches as if to say "Scratch me" and so I do. He is the happiest five-pound dog in the world. His false eye is milky in the sun, but his real eye is bright and brown and sparkly. I remember how traumatic his accident was, to him and to all of us. I flashback on his pain and the endless eye drops, and finally, the loss and replacement of his beautiful little eye, once so bright and real, with something dull and false.

He was traumatized. I was traumatized. Together we crawled through the days. His personality receded as his body went into survival mode to endure the pain. Once his eye was removed and his body recovered from surgery, he was (almost) back to his usual Scout-self within a month. I measured his return by the landmarks which are uniquely his. He runs full tilt through the house and then jumps across certain spots – from rug to rug, jumping over the hardwood floors and from our front porch across the metal welcome mat onto the rug in the hallway. Begging for dog treats and cocking his head from side to side as he listens to me talk, paying rapt attention to the pearls of wisdom that only he knows I am imparting to him. Sometimes it seems he's the only male around here who waits with baited breath for every fascinating word I say. When those traits which are uniquely and endearingly his came back, I knew Scout was back. Sometimes we call him One-Eyed Jack, but as far as we can tell, he doesn't take offense. Once his body healed, his spirit followed.

There's a lot to be said for a dog's approach to life.

Nothing fancy, just a sunspot. The only sunny spot in an otherwise unremarkable room and he is the embodiment of sublime contentment within it. How do dogs do that? It would be too easy to say that animals don't have the remarkable reasoning ability that we "higher" animals have, but looking at Scout, that doesn't seem like a rough trade off. He appears to be immersed in a moment of dog perfection. He sought out the perfect spot, lay his little self down in it and is soaking up the goodness of the moment. It's that which resonates so strongly with me. He is soaking up the goodness of the moment. The right here, right now, singular moment in time, he

is bathing his entire being in it. I hadn't been the only one struggling through the winter of 2011. Too many friends were suffering
through their own personal struggles and injuries and it weighed on
my heart. We all have our seasons of struggle. All around me people
I loved were seeking to quiet the storms that come and go into our
lives. Anxiety really wants to be our default mode. And yet, in the
infinitely wise words of God, written down for our eyes to seek and
to heal our hearts, we are counseled over and over to be anxious for
nothing. We are encouraged to live in the moment, and promised
that if we bring our cares to Him with prayer and praise, He hears the
cries of our hearts and cares for us. And yet, we struggle. We struggle
with anxiety, we struggle with doubt, we buckle and bend as our
storms come and go from our lives. Anxiety has a tenacious grip.

Be anxious for nothing. Look for sunspots. Carpe diem.
With those planted firmly in my mind, think what I could do. I
could act more like Scout.

We all have our own struggles which peak or recede. Leslie
was worried for her daughter who, at the too-young age of twenty-
two, had found a lump in her breast. We'd been trying to get together for a visit and had to keep cancelling on each other. The date we'd
agreed upon finally arrived, but then her daughter was waiting on her
diagnosis. I wasn't sure if my visit would be timely or appropriate.
Leslie said "Please, Shell, come, I could use your company" and so I
went. We laugh all the time when we're together. I can't imagine life
without her. She's funny and kind and lovely and hard on herself. It's
my obligation as her friend to agree with her and call her rude names,
out of love. One of the many beautiful things about old and dear
friends is sharing history. We've been absolute best friends since we
were sixteen. We had met at a party right after I'd moved back to my
old hometown and we'd just clicked. She was drinking beer out of a
boot mug and that sealed it. She doesn't even like beer, but she loved
the mug and we love cowboy boots so we became inseparable.

We shopped and ate and drank coffee and ate cookies and listened and talked and brought each other comfort and relief that only
such constancy of years can provide. We come at faith and belief in
a higher power from different directions, but we both agreed that life

can really wear you out without eyes lifted to a higher place. In many ways we are very different yet in all the important ways, very much the same. I tend to jump into and off things, and Leslie is more cautious and circumspect (and smarter). My mom called us the Odd Couple, after the old TV show. Odd maybe, but together we make a perfect complement. Our personalities combined make us a complete and perfect friend package.

We came to the shared conclusion, from very different life perspectives; life can grind you up and spit you out, so it's important to keep from running on fumes. Neither of us would ever win the Powerball lottery (we'd rather spend money on shoes). We talked about trying to keep that tank filled up with simple pleasures, like Scout was with his sunspot. Talking, shopping, and eating cookies isn't rocket science. We didn't solve anything and the realities of our worlds were still the same when I left to go home. I left her feeling lifted up and blessed, and her friendship and love had done the same for me. That day spent together filled us both up, imperfect lives and all.

I was her sunspot and she was mine. Thanks, Scout.

Chapter Thirty
Horse People

No philosophers so thoroughly comprehend us as dogs and horses.
Herman Melville

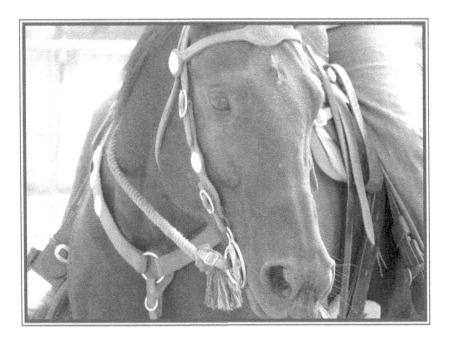

Horse people have always scared me a bit. And before anyone feels offended, I include myself in that category, so no hard feelings. You've gotta be just a little bit nuts to be in that category. There's no rational reason for pouring buckets of money into animals that poop it right out. Money spent not only on hay, but on supplements if you've got horses with any issues such as ulcers or a thousand other possibilities. Add special food for your old guys who need help keeping weight on in the winter. Shoes for some, trims for all, cute shirts for you and a myriad of other stuff like bits and blankets and saddles.

Much to Pat's chagrin, one saddle does not fit all and just might not fit anybody, sending you on a search for the perfect fitting saddle. If you have more than one horse, multiple this by the number of horses you have and it adds up fast.

Like I said, we're scary.

Horse people cover a pretty broad spectrum. Horses come in different breeds and sizes but then we start dividing them into lots of categories based on the activity we may want to do with them. Reiners, cutters, Western Pleasure, trail riders, gymkhana, ropers (calf and team), barrel racers, packers, bareback and saddle bronc, and we're just getting started. Moving over to our English saddle friends and you have hunters, jumpers, eventers, dressage, driving, endurance, hunting, and polo, to name a few. And the pasture pet. Pasture pet is the term for a horse that somehow scored the ultimate end game and wound up doing what some horses only dare dream about – lounging.

My first Aha! moment along my horsemanship journey was that my horse wasn't a vehicle to do an activity on. I'd grown up doing what we'd called "just riding." Shortly after this journey began I realized that any time spent with a horse is a learning experience, and usually for me. When I began to actually learn about the horse and our interaction with them, I met other women along the way who shared the same desire to learn. We've formed a tribe of horse people who are committed to this life-long pursuit of horsemanship. Thanks to them, their huge respect for the horse, and their combined knowledge, answers and encouragement are just a Facebook message away. Thanks to this tribe, I've been introduced to extraordinary horsemen and women who inspire me along this wondrous quest. Along the way the title "trainer" falls to the wayside and "horseman" becomes the norm. We aren't seeking to train. We're seeking to learn the language of the horse to improve our communication with them. We're learning to build solid horsemanship principles based on knowledge of the true nature of the horse. With the help of my horses' friends I'd searched for a horse to be my new partner, a partner that Steph qualified needed to be a "solid citizen." I found a mare named Satin in southern Oregon who checked all the boxes. My horse friend Patti lived nearby so she graciously went to check her out first and ride her for me. Satin gained everyone's approval and with Satin's help, I'd begin again.

The light went on big time when I met Harry Whitney thanks to Steph who's ridden with Harry for years. I signed up to take Satin to my first clinic since my wreck. Fortunately this clinic was at Melissa Windham's place and I knew I'd be among friends. The magnitude of being on horseback again was huge; gone were the days where I could throw on a saddle as I used to. It was a big deal being in a clinic setting again. There were a lot of new logistics: putting on all my new gear (body protector and helmet) and asking for help saddling up. Jeannie helped me get the trailer unhitched and Steph and Melissa helped me get ready. Auditors sat in double rows around the arena. It was packed. Usually having that many people watching is nerve-wracking, but I could feel them silently cheering me on from their fold-up chairs. Harry was kind and funny and by the end of our time he'd deemed Satin a solid citizen (confirming what we were all thinking). By the end of the clinic I felt like I could really do this. I don't know how it would have been possible without my own horse people who came alongside when I was feeling pretty beat up and helped me put it back together, piece by piece.

Harry focuses on the importance of having your horse's thought with you. Harry's horsemanship philosophy is summarized on his website where he shares "So often we focus on what the horse is doing, and miss the fact that the horse's mind will affect what he's doing and how he does it. If we give attention to the horse – how he is feeling in the moment, where his thought is and offer him the help he is looking for, many of the things we thought were problems will be cleared up." From hindsight I could see that if I had really set this in my mind before my ride with Wish, I would have cleared up her concerns rather than ignoring them and more than likely that day in late January would have turned out quite a bit differently.

Horsemanship is a quest and a journey. Every nugget of knowledge we pick up helps us to build the most positive relationship with our horses we can. The learning (and the journey) should never end.

Chapter Thirty-One

Year of the Snake

I'm not as good as I'm gonna get, but I'm better than I used to be
Tim McGraw

The rain and temperature began to fall at the same time. I was half way over the last grade before home, heading back from a much-awaited visit with Leslie. Pat called to tell me snow was predicted and I was hoping to get home before the skies opened up all the way. Incongruously, two men were pushing shopping carts laden with what I presumed was all they owned in the world up the steep grade of the highway as night began to fall. I berated myself for driving by, all the while wondering what exactly I would do if I had stopped. I didn't have a single dollar in my wallet. I did have two bags of dog food, a case of mangos, and six bottles of Costco margaritas, none of which seemed like they would be of any use to the bedraggled men. Even though I realized that stopping was probably not a good idea, it left an empty feeling in my heart as I drove on past. More than anything these last two years have left me with the knowledge that life can be pretty heartbreakingly hard. How they got there, literally and figuratively, I will never know. None of us start out thinking we'll end up pushing a grocery cart up a steep grade in the middle of nowhere.

It's rare that any of us end up where we thought we would.

Two years since my crash and burn. My neurosurgeon had said "You'll be 100% in a year," and I was dead-certain that he'd underestimated the remarkable powers of can-do. I've found out the hard way not once, but several times in my life, that sometimes even can-do can only do so much. No amount of will or perseverance changed the way I felt at the one year mark— and how I'd felt was pretty much pretty crappy. After that magic mile marker came and went, a lot of the steam went out of me. I had a couple of months where I really struggled. I was struggling with anxiety, trouble sleeping, and having what I guess could qualify as post-traumatic stress. Nights were hard. Busy days kept reality away, but as night settled so too did my reality which had been kept at bay but floated overhead during the day. I would drag myself to bed as late as possible and force myself to lie down. The quiet of night settled around me like an ominous whisper.

In the dark the hovering cloud would slowly descend to my chest where it would take a seat and the panic would set in. You know that feeling when something terrible has happened and you are finally able to sleep and when you awaken you have that brief moment where everything still feels okay? But when your mind fully wakes and you realize that yes, things are still terrible and your new reality wasn't just a bad dream? That. I felt that way in reverse —my new reality sat on my chest like an elephant I hadn't invited into bed with me. Twist and turn or hyperventilate, but there was no shaking the reality which was mine. I got messed up, and messed up bad. That was never going to change. No amount of positive thinking was ever going to change the fact that my back was a full-metal jacket of hardware.

There's only so much hyperventilating you can do until the person you sleep with wants to hold a pillow over your face. Fortunately it never got to that, but I know Pat felt helpless as he could feel my shoulders shaking in the dark, as I stuffed the corner of my pillow into my mouth and tried to outrun the demons of my damage. My reality floated above me, like warm air above cold. During the day I came and went and did what I did with only a few moments of harsh reality check throughout the day. I'd had stuff to do, animals and kids to feed. I just couldn't out run the nights. I can remember hyperventilating only once before, upon the loss of my sweet dog Courtney of my childhood. Now hyperventilating was kind of common to my nights and I was ashamed of myself for not being able to control my panic. I would say I have grit in the truest sense, but night stripped grit away from me, and I was left with the thinnest grip on peace. Only a few people asked and only a few knew that I still battled my accident a year after it had occurred. Part of my struggle was that working up to a year I had felt like perfect healing and "success'" were possible. It wasn't really so bleak until that milestone came and in spite of all my best efforts, I still felt like a fragment of my self. Until I could accept my new self as the real me, my struggle would continue.

High up in the hills, heading home, the radio reception was sketchy but I could still hear Tim McGraw singing *Standing in the rain so long has left me with a little rust, but put some faith in me and someday you'll see there's a diamond under all this dust.* It's lucky for me that God's hands never let go of me in spite of all the flailing around I'd done the past 716 days. Tim sings *I ain't as good as I'm gonna get, but I'm better than I used to be.* Praise God, you and me both, Tim. Even though the magical 365 days came and went, I still believe that I can continue moving to a place where my body doesn't feel so vulnerable, my mind doesn't feel such fear, and my spirit doesn't feel broken. I want to feel mended. I don't even think about wishing that none of this had ever happened anymore because I know that parts of me have become better for the journey. Strange maybe, but true. I look forward with the belief that as my busted body heals, my busted spirit will follow along.

I'd gone from 2011, The Chinese Year of the Rabbit, to the blur of 2012 The Year of the Dragon. The world was waiting to see if the Mayan calendar stuff held true and if the end was near. My only interest in the Mayan calendar conversation was that if the end was near, I really didn't need to worry about all this stuff. The world continued on and somehow another slow frustrating year had passed and it was now 2013, The Year of the Snake. My daily life in the country has had more than its fair share of run-ins with rattlers, so really every summer feels like the year of the snake. Two years had passed in a blur. I had dueling feelings like so much had happened and yet, not enough. Two years had felt like I was mired in quicksand, taking all of my commitment to pull my arms and legs out and make myself move forward. Yet at times, blissful times, the anxiety and fear were gone and replaced with an almost blinding sense of gratitude and of searing appreciation. I put those times into my heart to hold onto when the darker moments threatened to overtake me.

I remind myself; it ain't over till it's over. This wasn't a one-round rodeo. Just as Billy Etbauer's known for winning the tenth and last saddle bronc round of the National Finals Rodeo ten times, I too am hopeful for a big finish. Eight seconds might not seem like much, but multiply that by the ten days of the NFR and it's a lot. Some rounds he got bucked off, but he always finished big. We loved watching Billy ride because he gave it all he had every go-round and was known for being humble and generous out of the arena. Roughstock is a rough trade to be in. Those guys do it because they love it and probably because they're crazy – the rodeo joke is that the smart guys do the roping events and the crazy guys do the roughstock. Billy clinched his fifth title as the Oldest Roughstock World Champion in rodeo history in the Pro Rodeo Hall of Fame. He had a three decade career and made it to the NFR twenty-one of those years. I'm no Billy but like Billy, I ride because I love it. I just can't imagine never riding again. I don't watch rodeo anymore, but in rodeo and in life, I know every round counts. It ain't over till it's over. Billy showed me that.

Never in a million years did I think I'd find myself on the eve of two years later, still hurting, taking pony-rides on the oldest horse on our place. This journey has given a day at a time new meaning, but that's how I needed to do it. It's how we all need to do it. I had prayed during my anxious nights and finally one morning I woke with words that the Lord had put on my heart. He uses as few words as possible with me; probably because He knows that four words are the max I'm able to process. "Today you're good." Those few words helped me process all the anxiety and fear into one tiny sentence.

It's rare that any of us end up where we thought we would.

Six-year old me had confidently declared that grown-up me would be a veterinarian, comedian, and a tap dancer. I'm none of those things. Seemed like the lesson before me now was to figure out what this detour could teach me. Titanium and all. Fighting it wasn't helping me move forward from it. Fighting had been keeping me stuck to the spot where it all began. Today, I'm good. Four small words packed a big punch. None of us know the day or the time we'll breathe our last breath. Anything can happen on this spinning planet. Can and does. I'd seen enough to know in ICU.

But for me, right now, right here, on this day, I'm good.

Chapter Thirty-Two
If the Saddle Fits

The wind of heaven is that which blows between a horse's ears.
Arabian Proverb

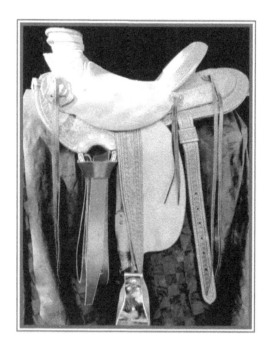

My horse friends are across the road, across the country, across the world. Through the wonder of the World Wide Web, we connect almost daily to say hey and, almost always, to laugh. We share the truth of our sometimes messy, sometimes wonderful lives sprinkled like glitter with both shit storms and miracles. I'm grateful that finding my way back to horses also brought me to a path crisscrossed with horse friends. We make up a multi-dimensional tribe: young, old, married, divorced, silly, and serious but all united by our love of the horse. Thanks to Ernie and Kitty who helped me find my way back, I also ended up finding my tribe. Shortly after they delivered Lickety Split to me, Ernie (an honest to goodness cowboy in this day and age) suggested I add another horse to my life. He knew I was on a horsemanship journey, and he recommended I find a nice two-year-old as it wouldn't have any bad habits. Ernie's words were truer than I had the sense to know at the time. Not too long after I bought a two-year old paint "pink" roan gelding out of Lakeview, Oregon, and began down the road of starting a horse. I named him Skeeter, since I'd bought him on the way back from the world-famous Paisley, Oregon, Mosquito Festival. My dad is a great partner in crime. He was driving and not very hard to convince, so thanks to him we made the detour and ended up heading home with a new horse. Turned out Ernie's observation was very true. Any hiccups Skeeter ended up with were just the ones I gave him. Starting a horse was a way bigger endeavor than I'd undertaken before. Skeeter was an almost blank slate, and I was getting ready to scribble all over it. Skeeter would be the proving ground of just how far my horsemanship was progressing. In spite of my fumbling rookie moves, Skeeter dealt with me more fairly than I deserved and we ambled along learning together.

Thanks to Skeeter, I met Stephanie at a women's horse camp. I'd just turned forty and was wondering what the heck had happened to my thirties. It seemed like the perfect time to celebrate that monumental shift in decades with my first horse clinic. Summers are fun for non-farmers, but if you're in the business, summers can be pretty brutal. Summer is make it or break it time. Summer is our busiest season, so for me to go to an August clinic was no small deal. Making this happen involved driving the boys to Oregon, driving the five plus hours back home to northern California, loading up the trailer and Skeeter, and driving four hours through winding mountain roads to the clinic. I'd already spent the best part of two days just getting back and forth from Oregon before hitting the road again. After all this back and forthing I ended up being the last person to arrive at the week-long clinic. I introduced myself to the group by immediately driving right past the turn-off in our crew cab and gooseneck stock trailer; requiring an eighteen-point turn on a very narrow road to get turned back around, which provided great entertainment for the nine other women watching from the porch.

After this first mortifying how do you do, I unloaded Skeeter and went into the rustic cabin, only to find that rustic meant there were no actual beds. I was kind of used to sleeping in a bed so I'd failed to bring any kind of pad to soften the hardness between the floor and my sleeping bag. My roommate was Stephanie. I learned quickly that Steph had just passed her bar exam and that Steph is an excellent sleeper. I was so jacked up on the fact that I'd actually done this – I was actually at a clinic – I couldn't sleep. Jacked up for sure, but sleeping on a hard floor wasn't helping. It didn't bother Steph at all, a fact which both annoyed and impressed me.

The next day we all headed out to get our horses saddled up and head out to the arena. I gathered up my nerve. Skeeter and I entered the arena which prompted my previously calm horse to start bucking like a full-on saddle bronc across the entire arena on a perfect diagonal. Apparently I gained cred by riding him the full distance, and if I recall correctly, with one arm in the air just like Billy Etbauer. This turned out to be my first lesson in the importance of proper saddle fit. I hadn't come across that lesson yet in my horseman-ship journey and was still using my saddle from high school which I quickly learned (to my compounding mortification) didn't fit Skeeter properly. Many years later, many of us from that first clinic are still friends and my introduction to the group never fails to be funny. Well, at least they think so. How to make an entrance—I've got that one covered.

Fast forward some years and many miles of knowledge. When Satin came into my life, she looked exactly like the perfect black imaginary horse I'd spent drawing my entire year of third grade. Satin is a true black: the black mare little girls dream about. She has a few assorted white feet and a white spot on her withers which im-mediately told me that she too had had a run in with bad saddle fit. The white stands out in stark contract on her black, and I made her a promise that our partnership would involve a saddle which fit her perfectly. Pat was on board as he was invested in making sure I had everything set up as optimally as possible when I started to ride again.

I researched saddle makers and saddle fit, and I asked my horse friends for their input. Thanks to Mark and Crissi I came to know Gary Winkler, saddle maker out of Coeur d'Alene, Idaho. I loved Mark's WS saddle and how meticulous Gary was in the craftsmanship of the outside of the saddle as well as the tree. Gary worked with custom saddle tree makers Rod and Denise Nikkel of Alberta. Gary is a super nice guy as I found out when we began working together on Satin's new saddle. I pestered him pretty much daily with my ideas and pictures and designs. I pestered him daily with measurement questions. He never even pretended like he wasn't home when I'd call. I'd chosen Gary for his attention to the fit. The most important thing was that this saddle fit Satin properly, of course, but once you start heading down the path of having that very likely once in a lifetime opportunity to create a saddle from scratch, well. Very quickly every beautiful tooled tidbit you've ever seen and all the pictures you didn't know you had in your head come pouring out. I'd seen a tooling pattern called Vaquero Lace somewhere and had fallen in love with it so we worked off that to design the main pattern. Gary would send me samples and we'd tweak them until one day (to Gary's relief, no doubt) I knew that was it. My only other request was no daffodils and yes sunflowers and Gary got busy. Gary is a heck of a good sport.

The day my saddle arrived was better than ten Christmases rolled into one. It still looks as new as a baby, but Satin and I are slowly adding miles to it.

Skeeter, I still miss you.

Chapter Thirty-Three
Scars

A really strong woman accepts the war she went through and is ennobled by her scars.
Carly Simon

We all have them. Some are easy for the world to see, but others are trickier to detect, like those that tore our souls and blew holes in our hearts and hide silently out of sight unless we choose to make them known. Fresh and vivid or old and faded, both leave their mark on our lives. They mark us up like the road map of a journey which may have been the one we had planned but much more often, from a detour we didn't see coming.

I've been thinking about scars a lot lately. It's been a scar-filled few years. The first sight of my new scar wrenched my heart. I could hardly bear to look at it. Since it's not going anywhere, I'd been struggling to come to terms with it. I'm working on moving it from a painful place in my heart —a reminder of who I once was and what had happened - to a place of reconciliation. And maybe someday, hopefully, to a place of wisdom. It's been a slow process, but I'm getting there. Fortunately, it's true what people say about time and healing. My two major medical issues of note have left behind physical scars: the faded scar from the emergency caesarean section bringing my eldest son into the world and this new and most visible scar from where they removed my rib to repair my back.

It's a surprisingly small scar considering all the action that went on in there. One surgeon opened me up, passed the job to the two neurosurgeons and the five nurses who made up the surgical team. After five days of waiting, the day finally came. There's really no way to describe the cold blast that hits your veins when someone finally says "It's time to go." Surgery prep was a mad surge of people intent on their individual tasks. My only job was to count backward from 10, 9, 8. I got the easy job. That's a lot of people who have seen me naked, and I don't even know their names, except for one of the nurses whose name was Bob. My last thought before I lost consciousness was that someone would draw a smiley face on my butt. I blame the drugs. Nine hours later I woke to someone gently calling my name. Maybe it was Bob. Pat was waiting in the hallway as they finally wheeled me out. He was very emotional to see me after the long surgery. I looked up at him lovingly and said "Honey, I'd like to introduce you to Bob." Again: it was the drugs.

I give props to my neurosurgeons Dr. Elden Eichbaum and Dr. Alan Hunstock and orthopedic surgeon Dr. Eric Schmidt who opened me up and removed my rib so that it could be ground up and placed in the titanium bone cage to act as a bone graft to create a spinal fusion. They had a big discussion as to how large the initial incision should be. Dr. Eichbaum lobbied for smaller, for which I am eternally grateful. I appreciate their desire to minimize the invasiveness of the procedure. Many back surgeries require entry from the back itself but in my case they used a lateral access so only my left side is scarred. My scar memento is all of four inches long. I've no idea how they did so much in such a little incision. The first time I ran my hand along my side and found a genuine dent from the lack of my rib, was more than a little bit disturbing. The dent was proof of the reality of the new me: minus one rib but plus hardware.

Our society doesn't embrace scars. We are pressed to seek perfection. Many cultures mark their bodies reverently with ink as rites of passage to celebrate transitions. Our pervasive media deluges us with a proffering of perfection and youth, diverting us from celebrating our life metamorphoses. Scars can be tough to show to the world, if we see them as imperfection rather than our visible story. Scars tell the truth, something we can be loath to do with ourselves and others. It's scary. It's hard to lose a parent when you're a kid as I did, and sometimes it isn't until you are an adult that you realize that loss left a deep hole in your heart. My relationships with my kids, horses, and dogs have helped heal my unseen scars. Their innate honesty and genuineness has filled those holes life poked in my soul.

Scars can be our own star chart, points of navigation reminding us where we came from and guiding us toward our new direction.

Looking at the scars that mark my skin, some make me smile and help me to believe that perhaps someday I will look at the scar on my side the same way. My favorite scar is on my right index finger from the alligator lizard that got away. It helps me see ten-year-old me, all knees and braids and crazy for animals, still devastated from the death of my father the year before, and learning to live with that grief in a child's way. Animals were my happy space and I surrounded myself with them. I'd have made a great Noah. I'd made a trap to catch that lizard but in my enthusiasm I had grabbed him rather than let the trap do its work. Alligator lizards are ill-tempered and very flexible. It took lots of shaking to get him dislodged from my finger. That scar reminds the much older me about the much younger me and makes me smile.

My C-section scar brings back memories of graduate school,

newly-married and commuting an hour each way. I was finally kicking some major academic butt and finishing my thesis. My scar reminds me of my water breaking six weeks early as I'd returned home late one night and the endless hours of oxytocin-induced labor that followed. I can still recall the metallic taste of the pain; the manufactured contractions as constant as waves crashing onto the shore. It reminds me of when we realized that no matter how hard I labored, he wasn't going to come along on his own. But more than the pain preceding it, my scar reminds me of the love that flooded my soul the first moment I saw my son. That love hit me with a force so powerful I would have never believed such intensity possible until I had felt it for myself. I look at that scar now and I feel only love, not the pain. I know it can be done.

I look at this new scar and try to integrate its story into my life without regret. It deserves to be seen with acceptance and even joy that in spite of being literally broken in half; I can walk and ride again. It tells my story just like the others. I can't Whiteout it gone. I don't want to. They're the black Sharpie lines tracing the outline of my life. We don't get to travel through life unscathed. My scars are helping to teach me that it's how we live with and because of them. It's not just the external scars that need our tending. We can ignore those scars people can't see in the mistaken belief that out of sight, out of mind. Those are the tough ones. I'm trying to turn the scars on my spirit into reminders of how blessed I am in spite of, and because of.

One Sunday our pastor was speaking about how Jesus was broken, physically and spiritually, during crucifixion. As he spoke I saw with new eyes a flesh and blood man, fractured in every way possible. Something about his words that morning struck right through my heart. He painted a living picture of the sacrificial life Jesus had walked up until that day; a life emptied of self and filled instead with the love of a servant's true heart. I'd felt like my brokenness had relegated me to the discard pile, like worn-out clothes to be given away. Those words that Sunday opened my heart to ways my brokenness could be used in ways I'd never imagined. In ways my unbroken self would have never understood. My self had so often gotten in the way of my spiritual life. How I thought things should be, how I saw my life unfolding. The pastor's words reverberated in my heart. As we walked out the doors into the sunlight I felt washed by a sense of understanding and purpose I'd almost given up finding.

His ways are not our ways.

I think of kintsugi "to patch with gold," the Japanese art of repairing broken pottery with a lacquered resin which looks like veins of gold. Kintsugi is called the art of broken pieces. The mended item will never look the same and the golden resin is a beautiful reminder of the break. Its brokenness is revealed and the beauty inherent in the repair honored. Much of the art of kintsugi is fueled by the Japanese concept of wabi-sabi. Wabi is said to embrace simplicity and sabi, the beauty to be found in wear and in age. If only we look; if only we look with new eyes. We may choose to see these mends as a kind of homage to our life's journey. Our outer being dims with life and time, whether we accept that or not. Our inner being can grow to be more beautiful than we'd imagined if we treat our scars as opportunities to become more expansive than our unscarred selves. I had struggled to accept my truth, and had been led (and sometimes dragged kicking and yelling) to a new vantage point where I could see beyond my own construct. The things I'd valued about myself before were being refashioned through newly opened eyes and a renewed heart. Now I could see that my own "mend," just like kintsugi, could be my reminder that there was beauty in broken things.

The science geek in me goes back to more familiar terrain. I'm reminded of the First Law of Thermodynamics – energy cannot be created or destroyed, but only transformed. This journey has transformed me. Physically I'm definitely worse for wear, but the glimpse I've had of the transformative power of love more than makes up for that. A while back I'd posted a picture of me wearing my old western hat. The hat band is so worn it is practically torn in the middle. It's held together by only atoms and space dust. I'd asked my friends "New hatband or keep the old?" No one thought I should replace the hatband. They loved the hat. It's torn and it's worn, but they all saw the beauty in the story the hat told.

I will keep on keeping on the work to view my scars as beautiful veins of gold running through my life's story. They are telling my story too, all of it – the good, the bad, the ugly, and the beautiful. I will challenge myself each day to choose to honor it.

And, yep, I'm keeping the old hatband.

Chapter Thirty-Four
Broken Is Not My Story

Don't move the way fear makes you move.
Move the way love makes you move.
Move the way joy makes you move.
Osho

None of us go looking for traumatic experiences to see if we too can rise like the phoenix from the ashes. We're drawn to stories of redemption, but that doesn't mean we want to be the star of that story. Some circumstances act like speed bumps, a 5 mph slowdown, but then there are those that feel like we slammed into the wall doing

90. I didn't go looking for an accident, but I got one.

God's been patiently reminding me that He's not a God of circumstance. I've framed my reality by my circumstances far too often, but He isn't bound by circumstance. I was literally broken into halves and put back together thanks to my neurosurgeons' audacity and with the help of titanium, Ti, element 22 on the Periodic Table. My concept of self was also broken, but that wasn't something they could fix in the operating room. When I began this journey, broken was a place I wanted to be far away from. I had no idea how to put the pieces back together. I began writing to chronicle the small joys that were scattered around this path, to remind myself that they were indeed there. When they were written down, they began to feel real. They began to feel like they made a difference.

I'd fully imagined that within the year that my neurosurgeon had proclaimed, I'd be 100% again. People asked how I was doing and my confident reply was "I'll be better than before." How ignorant I feel looking back on those days. I don't know who I was trying to convince, but at the time I believed it. When I began I thought I could already see the ending. Within a year I was sure I'd have fought the rabbit and won; but that wasn't how things unfolded. The challenge turned out to be quite a bit different. I soon realized it was to become a long journey. I never imagined it would take two years rather than the half year I'd over-optimistically predicted to get to a point where I could sleep peacefully at night, let alone feel put back together.

If I'd known at the beginning just how long my journey would be, I would have packed differently.

Accidents seem to be split into two: the accident and the aftermath. Leslie and I were talking recently about trauma, and how you just don't know the breadth of it until, well, until you know the breadth of it. The aftermath has been much harder than I ever anticipated. My wreck broke more than my back. Where I'd been strong, I was weak and where I'd been independent, I was vulnerable. To be brutally honest, I felt more than broken, I felt almost irretrievably lost. Wrestling with my new reality, I kept looking to find a way back to who I had been. It took many, many more days than that year before I would realize that going back was not an option. Who I had been was gone, blown apart, just like my L1.

Black Sharpie lines stay put no matter what you try to erase them with. If your little kids have ever gotten ahold of one, you already know this too well. My unexpected dismount wasn't my first black Sharpie line. My father died just months before my ninth birthday. I didn't know it was coming, but it came and changed my life irrevocably. Losing my dad shaped me in powerful ways which I didn't understand at the time. I can remember bits and pieces of the after-math: sitting in the front row of the church during his funeral and turning around to look at the sea of people and feeling a wave of coulda, shoulda, wouldas. They knew things that as a child I did not. Many of them had known that he had battled with his illness for years and were awash in their own regrets of visits not made, words not said. (I've been blessed with not one, but two, wonderful dads – one just got me when I was twelve). I learned early that nothing is forever, and that we take things for granted at our own risk. These two black Sharpie lines are kind of like my life's bookends. Black Sharpie lines are hard to absorb when you're little. They're not all that much easier to absorb when you're big.

Even with that ruthless early life lesson, I forget. Every so often I need a reminder that our moments are not to be squandered. Our small rural community was recently ravaged by wildfires so deadly they defied control. The fires decimated our county two summers in a row, leaving it physically and emotionally burnt. Survivors wondered how they'd emerged untouched and felt the guilt that survivors often do. Those who'd lost everything were forced to dig down deep inside to find what little tatters they had left to start again, to say goodbye, and to search for peace to survive each day after. We all mourned. The acrid smell of grief mixed with the smell of ash lingering in the air. One evening I went out to feed and a charred scrap of paper landed in my hand like an ashen snowflake. The words on the paper were still clear, and only the edges were singed; a ghostly and holy reminder of how quickly all can turn to dust.

We were some of the lucky ones. We loaded up our vehicles as one fire threatened to blow up as the others had, but somehow it was snuffed out before turning into the same kind of monster we'd watched the others become. Watching the black billowing smoke just a stone's throw from our property we loaded up the few things that we'd decided to take. The smoke crystallized my realization that I had all I needed in the back of a truck. Our family was safe, our dogs loaded up, the horses were ready for the trailer. So many others didn't get that chance. Making the list of what you would bring with you if you could is clarifying: animals first and then our memories, some boots, and horse gear. My list mirrored the constants, the lights on this journey as well: my family, friends, the dogs and horses. Make your own list. You'll find that when pencil hits paper, the things that matter most rise quickly to the surface and the rest just falls away.

So much was falling away from me. From the things I'd thought I couldn't live without, couldn't "be" without. When the realization hit me that summer Sunday that Jesus was broken for busted up me, detours and all; I realized on a cellular level how much I was loved, and that that love had nothing to do with what I could do or how strong I was. It was unconditional, and without any merit on my part. I stopped fighting the brokenness and tried to absorb it. I tried to put down the old hand mirror that I was used to holding up to reflect back: Strong – check; capable – check. I held the now-shattered pieces of that mirror. Would they ever go back together like they once had? No. In spite of how much I wanted them to, it wasn't possible. Was that even how I was supposed to rebuild my life? This new mirror showed me things I'd never even dreamed of, like what a servant's heart really looks like. A heart empty of self, a love not based on strength of body but forged in heavenly fire.

It look much longer than I'd thought and much longer than I'd wanted it to, but in so many ways I've come out on the other side. Broken isn't my only story; it's a part of my life's story. Occasionally I've seen glimpses of the beauty that comes from a love like that through the new and improved emptied-out me, and it makes me hunger for more.

Reliving that first year of intense recovery if it were laid out in front of me again isn't something I'd ever want to have to face, and I pray I don't ever have to. Once was enough. Sometimes at night I see a flash of what it must look like inside my body, and the old anxiety rises up so fast that it catches my heart unaware and it clenches. I can hear that elephant whispering, and I breathe and I remind myself that today, I'm good. Sometimes in the deepest hours of the night the elephant waiting patiently over the bed offers to come and land on my chest again, but now (at least most nights) I am able to tell it to take a hike.

There have been so many unexpected blessings as well. My family, friends, and my faith lifted up my spirit and my heart. The outpouring of love filled my heart to overflowing. It filled up spaces I knew existed and some I hadn't been aware of. I find encouragement and strength in my favorite Scripture that promises me *all things work together for the good....* Not just some things, but all things. This whole experience would be for naught if I didn't believe that God has a plan for the new me. The remodeled me, and that I can be a better human being because of it, rather than in spite of it.

And I thank God for reminders. One night while I was doing chores, my eye caught sight of a rusty half a horse shoe, buried by all but a tiny end. I love rusty things so I dug it out and set it on the weathered railroad tie. Was it a rusty piece of junk or a gentle reminder? I like to believe it was a well-timed reminder: a reminder of my love of horses, of these new lessons and how weathering (the horse shoe's and my own) add a patina to ordinary things which, through the eyes of the beholder, can make them extraordinary. This journey has helped me learn to cherish those ordinary things which remind me they often hold extraordinary within them. I'm grateful to all the animals big and small who crisscrossed my path and brought with them these lessons and joys along this unexpected journey. Their sweet presence and gentle reminder of the beauty and seasonality of life added bursts of color when all I could see were those black Sharpie lines. They brought magic with them, where, and when, I'd needed it. Our world is full of hurt, but it is also full of hope. I found mine through the love of my family, the steadfastness of my friends, the grounding power and unconditional love of my dogs. I found hope through my abiding love for the majestic horse, which stayed in my heart even when it was broken. I found hope in my faith which promises me that even though in the moment I may not be able to see it, in the end, all things in my life can work together for the good.

48,000 hours, 2,880,000 minutes. Two thousand days have passed since an unfortunate dismount started me on this journey of wreck, wonder, and recovery. It feels like a lifetime, and yet it's a blink, really. A journey of infinite steps: the first taken after my titanium back was created and a thousand others forward on this unexpected journey filled with both immense sadnesses and untold joys. Unexpected teachers and lessons have decorated that path, as unexpected yet welcome as seeing a falling star or being dusted with snow in April. My late afternoon ride has come full circle two thousand days later. I'm ready to say goodbye to broken. I'm looking forward to a new journey. My journey began with The Year of the Rabbit and ends at The Year of the Rooster. In Chinese astrology, roosters are said to be the most motivated of all the animals. I am motivated to close this chapter and begin a new chapter. Not long ago I was listening to a radio program where a man was speaking about his twelve-year battle with cancer. He said his cancer had long been declared incurable, and while cancer is his burden, it isn't his story. Out loud I say "Amen," a spoken encouragement, to him, and to myself.

The winter after my wreck I had the privilege of attending the Legacy of Legends in Las Vegas. Legacy of Legends is a tribute to the horsemanship of Ray Hunt, started by his wife Caroline and his sons, grandchildren, and friends. I watched Buck Brannaman help out an extremely troubled high level hunter-jumper who was so petrified of anything that moved he could hardly function if touched. It wasn't pretty. That horse was used to going through the motions, and doing it at a high level. He was doing it; but out of his mind with fear if anything unexpected crossed his path. At one point the horse did something that amused the crowd and Buck chided us for laughing. He said "There's nothing funny about the way this horse feels." The crowd fell silent and I think in that moment we all realized what an obligation we have to the horses we encounter. Buck did what it took to help that horse and he said something that has stuck in my mind. He said, "My goal is to help this horse feel like life is a fair deal."

I love that. It says it all about horsemanship and the kind of relationship worth building with horses. Having friends who understand the call of the horse kept me afloat when I couldn't find my way out by myself. Giving myself permission to fail I've also come to realize I make fewer things once called mistakes and many more things that feel like discoveries, in horsemanship and in life. My ground driving may never look like the fluid dance Mark Rashid has with horses, but I damn well don't look like a chicken. I'll take progress wherever I can get it, in horsemanship and in life.

So I guess you could say the rabbit started it all, but really, I think it was the horse. My love for the horse has never dimmed. That love gave me the desire to ride again. Each time I throw my leg back over the saddle, I can feel those broken parts come back together. Someday soon I hope there aren't many left. I've learned more from horses and dogs through this journey than they've ever learned from me. Their authenticity helped keep my compass pointed to true north when it threatened to head south. Today I'm good. My hardware hasn't gone haywire, my family is safe. Each day I remind myself to take a deep breath, say a prayer of gratitude, and keep looking heavenward. None of us know the day or time of our last day and anything can happen on this spinning planet. But for me, right now, on this day, I'm good.

Buck has said, "Horses and life, it's all the same to me." I agree. I know I'm not the first person to ever fall off a horse, and I know I won't be the last. If my story helps you stay on, or get back on, that's good enough for me.

It might not be a horse you fall off, but no matter what throws you, I hope you get back on.

About the Author

Michelle Scully earned her B.S. in Zoology and a M.S. in Biology with an Ecology emphasis. She's been a university-researcher, DJ, college administrator, black jack dealer, biology instructor, and stay-at-home mom to her two sons. She's had more than a few adventure-related broken bones and has finally figured out the cause and effect. She and her family are part of a multi-generational family farming operation in northern California. She loves horses and her husband too, just like the Tom Petty song. This is her first book.

Simba's kindness got me back in the saddle,
and Satin and I are taking it from there.